M000286143

10

THINGS I WISH

MY Father

WOULD HAVE

Taught ME

10

THINGS I WISH

My Father

WOULD HAVE

Taught ME

Tony Hall Sr.

10 Things I Wish My Father Would Have Taught Me

Copyright © 2015 by Anthony Q. Hall, Sr.

All rights reserved. No part of this book may be reproduced, distributed, or transmitted in any form or by any means, including photocopying, recording, or other electronic or mechanical methods, without prior written permission from the author.

Scripture quotations are taken from the Holy Bible, New Living Translation, copyright ©1996, 2004, 2007, 2013 by Tyndale House Foundation. Used by permission of Tyndale House Publishers, Inc., Carol Stream, Illinois 60188. All rights reserved.

Other Scripture references are from the following sources:

New King James Version® Copyright © 1982 by Thomas Nelson. Used by permission. All rights reserved.

The Message Copyright © by Eugene H. Peterson 1993, 1994, 1995, 1996, 2000, 2001, 2002. Used by permission of Tyndale House Publishers, Inc.

Scripture taken from the NEW AMERICAN STANDARD BIBLE®, Copyright © 1960,1962,1963,1968,1971,1972,1973,1975,1977,1995 by The Lockman Foundation. Used by permission.

Cover designed by New Spectrum Media

Author's Photo by Bleusol Photography

Published by Anthony Q. Hall, Sr.

Edited by Jossalyn's Journey (www.jossalynsjourney.com)

10 Things I Wish My Father Would Have Taught Me
CONTENTS

FOREWORD

Allow me to introduce myself. Who I am is not important--what I am is. I am a son. I am a man, made better by the wisdom of a man dedicated to God. As a man who had no strong relationship with his earthly father I was unaware of the power within me. It took a great man to see and understand the greatness of another man. Bishop Hall unlocked the door to the man I am today, by the wisdom of God. I am forever grateful for my spiritual father. The psalmist said wisdom is the principal thing and with all thy getting get an understanding. Wisdom indeed is what you will receive in your time spent with this writing. His humor will tickle you. His honesty will shock you. His revelations will deliver you. Hear now, the mind of a man made by God, whose wisdom is from God. The Bible declares that we have thousands of instructors but we have not many fathers. I am concerned about the lack of fathering in this day. I am concerned about men who have no relationship with their father. These men are often misguided missiles creating destruction. Great fathers shoot the arrows of their sons towards the bull's-eye of their purpose by teaching, training and correcting them. This is the blessing of a father. Now, receive direction, instruction and guidance as you read on in Jesus' name.

Pastor David L Johnson
Men of Integrity

FOREWORD

Our world is inundated with images and illusions. Things and people look good on the outside, but once you peel back the layers you find that things and people aren't always as they seem. Pastor Tony has managed to masterfully mirror the stories of so many of us who have struggled with a longing to be nurtured, loved, and affirmed by our fathers. Some of us are married with children, still trying to find the center of ourselves. On paper, this desire seems simple...nominal even, but in real-life, the weight of this craving shoves us to find relief in unhealthy ways. It looks good, but it's not good.

The wisdom Pastor Tony shares in *10 Things I Wish My Father Would Have Taught Me* answers many of the questions that have plagued the lives of successful, yet broken (adult) children. He reminds us that it is possible for our families to live healthy once we are healed. Through his personal testimony, and the testimonies of those he has counseled, he helps us to eliminate our excuses. He challenges each of us to become brave, and finally confront, and conquer our fears.

This book is a picture of hope rising. It is filled with truth and instruction. You will see yourself on the pages, and for me there's something liberating about this notion. To me, it says, "I was not the only one. We aren't the only ones."

As you continue to read and turn the pages, you will see what is possible for each us—victory. Pastor Tony is winning in life, although he had to learn some of the lessons the hard way. If winning is possible for him, as you turn the page to start the book, please know winning is possible for you.

Winning is possible for us.

Stacey Joseph Harris
Lead Coach and Mentor
Project Passion Mentoring Institute
Dallas, TX
www.projectpassionmentoring.com

ACKNOWLEDGMENTS

Who would have thought a year ago I would finally finish my first book?

I am amazed by the things that happen when you have incredible people in your life who push you past your comfort zone.

First, I want to send love and appreciation to Maceo and Stacey Harris. From our time together, last December, you helped me understand how the things I purposely shared with you would have so much value in written format. I must admit, I doubted that you knew what you were talking about, but your love and support has brought out what you saw and heard in me. Denise and I are so appreciative to you both for hearing and seeing something in me. You refused to let me quit. More books are on the way.

Second, I want to thank my kids, Darrell Alexander, Anthony Hall Jr., Felicia Bramwell, and April Hall for your constant support. Special thanks to April for being my rock when I was tired and discouraged; you were also my mother when I needed a strong nudge to step up my game. You are the apple of my eye, and the reason that some of my thoughts made it to the pages of this book.

I want to thank God for Conquerors Shield of Faith International, no pastor has it better than I do. You prayed with me when I didn't want to write another chapter. Thank you for being my prayer warriors during this process. I'm the richest man in the world because I have such an amazing church family. I love you dearly.

Thank you to all of my spiritual children all over the world. I especially want to thank Pastor Sherri Fuller and Pastor David

Johnson. Sherri, you came into our lives 30 years ago, and helped me become the spiritual father I am today. Although I was young and hard to deal with, you are the harvest of my years of faithful fathering. David, you are on so many pages in this book. As a spiritual son, you taught me lessons that we laugh about today.

Lastly, to my wife of 38 years, Denise Hall, thank you for your love and support while writing this book. I have preached to thousands of people, I have prayed for hundreds of thousands of people, but I have never felt the strain of anything like writing this book.

Denise, you have heard these stories for 30 years, and you still acted as if you were hearing them for the first time. Who I am, and who I've become, is because your hand and heart gently guide me while doing what God has called me to do. Most people never hear of the impact they make in the world, but every day I try to tell you how valuable you are to this world. Our world is better; I am better because of your love and support.

I know when I have written my 10th book, your smile and support will be there. I know you will continue to push me beyond my imagination, and when we leave this world, we will be empty with nothing else to say.

Until then, I thank my Heavenly Father for sending me His best angel. Denise Hall, that angel is you!

INTRODUCTION

When you buy a new product, most times you cannot wait to get home, tear open the box, and commence to enjoying what you've purchased. If you are wise, the first place you go is to the user's guide to figure out the features you have, and the best way to utilize the product. You may even keep the user's guide handy for a small period of time until you are fully comfortable.

I can imagine the entrance into parenthood can foster the same type of excitement. You watch your child develop over a nine month period, and then you hold them in your arms and realize that he or she belongs to you. You may even begin to anticipate all of the future experiences you will share. However, this scenario is quite different; you don't get a user's guide with your new child. Even with the research you have conducted, you quickly figure out that being a parent is trial and error. Every child is different, and any previously conceived parenting views can change drastically.

Some have had great experiences with their own parents, while others may not reflect positively on their parental relationships. In this moment, you must make an important decision. Will you model your past experience, or will you forge your own path?

As the daughter of Bishop Tony Hall, Sr., I have witnessed so many great days, but I have also experienced some not so great days. In my younger years, I had no idea the pain behind the love my father displayed for his children. With time, I learned of the struggles my father faced as a young child and throughout most of his formative years. It caused me to better understand his journey. Not having a cookie-cutter parental relationship meant he was determined to have better for his children. Some of his methods worked and others...not so much (LOL)! Nevertheless, he was willing (with the help of God) to keep trying. This book has been years in the making; it is truly a labor of love. I believe my dad is willing to expose his own scars to help heal and transform the lives of others.

This isn't another how-to handbook; it is a "user's guide" of sorts. These pages contain real-life experiences, revelations, and wisdom to help you heal, learn, and grow. I encourage you to take some time with each chapter. Allow the words captured on these pages to not only guide you, but also change you. Don't be afraid to read and re-read the sections that resonate strongly with you because those may be the very areas that need some special attention in your life. More than anything, I hope you realize that you hold the key to having a different life, and I believe this book will be the catalyst to get the process started for you.

Dad, your baby girl is so proud of you. God knows getting you to sit down and stay focused long enough to put your thoughts on paper is a miracle indeed (LOL). I will never forget the times you called me after writing a chapter and read it to me in tears. I hope you are aware of the lives you have and will continue to change during your lifetime. You, sir, are rich because your wealth goes far beyond the dollars in your pocket. Your labor of love is not in vain. Keep striving and pushing with the assurance that when you do leave this Earth (prayerfully not anytime soon), you will leave fully poured out—a vessel used by the Master.

April N. Hall

CHAPTER 1

FATHERS HURT TOO

My relationship with my father is best described as difficult. Although I carried his last name, there were so many things about him that I didn't understand. He was the hero of my heart, and the enemy of my soul.

MY FATHER'S STORY

Clarence Albert Hall was born November 11, 1933. In 1933, life for a black man in Georgia was incredibly hard. My father's life was colored by tragedy, success, loss, racial tension, injustice, and honor.

His mother was a severe alcoholic. His father was a very passive man who lived on his wife's family plantation. He had to drop out of school in the third grade to help take care of a very dysfunctional family, yet he was the youngest child. At the age of 19 he met Florine, my mother. Her father was mentally unstable and later committed to a mental institution. During this time my mother and father married because my grandfather otherwise would not allow them to date. After they married my mother's father was released from the mental institution, and she and my father moved to Pontiac, Michigan in hopes of a better life.

Having seven children and helping his siblings settle in Detroit, my father decided to leave Pontiac and move to Detroit. After moving to Detroit, my parents devised a plan to work hard and provide for their kids. My father worked three jobs, while my mother worked to make our home very comfortable. Everything was flowing as planned until the last week of August, 1966.

Early one morning after taking my father to work, my mother fell asleep at the wheel of the car. The phone rang and the news my father received on the other end of the phone changed our lives forever. About two weeks later, my mother—his wife was gone. Dead at 33 years old. Their plan did not include single parenting, but now he had to raise seven children alone.

As an adult I began to realize that my father, my hero, was wounded in battle. However, growing up, I didn't realize that Clarence Hall was a man full of hurt, and a great deal of pain. He needed help.

My father was hurting.

MANAGING EXPECTATIONS

Several years ago while talking to my youngest daughter April, I started to express my frustration surrounding the actions of a person who asked for my help. Once again, I shared wisdom for their problem and although my counsel was solicited, the person rejected my advice. Their actions agitated me. I didn't ask to help them. They asked for my help. My daughter has a way of smacking me with my own words. She told me something that shifted my perspective.

She said, "Daddy, you have great wisdom, and people's lives are changed if they choose to listen, but some people will choose not to take heed to your wisdom and that's okay. Share your wisdom with others, but remove the expectation of them applying what you've shared. Number one, it's their problem, and their problems do not belong to you. Stop having the expectation that people will follow your advice, and let people choose what they are willing to follow. And, once they make a choice, do not take it personally."

Our conversation caused me to consider a new school of thought. In reality everyone finds their place in life based upon life experiences, lessons learned along the way, family upbringing, and personal philosophies that are unique to them. Because we live different lives, our expectations may be different from person to person. From this awareness, I developed a way to relate to others based on levels of expectation. My method is not systematic; it's intuitive, and determined with wisdom.

Now, whether in marriage counseling, life coaching, family coaching, pastoral coaching, or the investment that I make into my spiritual sons and daughters, I classify them based on where they are at this moment in their life. I've developed an internal scale ranging from Level 1 to Level 10 that assigns each person a number (Level 1 being the lowest and level 10 being the highest). Take for example Benji, Brenda, and Derrick. Three different people. Each person had issues with their father, and each dealt with the issue differently.

BENJI: EXPECTATION LEVEL 1

As we sat in my office, I opened the conversation with Benji the way I start my conversations with everyone.

I asked, "Will you tell me about your father?"

In asking Benji, the look on his face was one of shock, as he didn't expect me to ask that question.

As he looked down, Benji said what so many other people have said when I've asked that very important question.

He took a deep breath, looked at me and said, "I don't know where my father is. The last time I saw him I was either 10 or 12 twelve years old. He showed up to our house Christmas Day."

The smile that came over Benji's face soon turned into anger as Benji recalled how great that day was.

"My father helped me put together my toys, even told me he loved me and how he would always be there for me. Just as quickly as he came, poof, he was gone. I remember hearing my mother and grandmother telling my dad, "do not to let that boy down again." My father promised, but I haven't seen him since that day."

Disappointed, Benji turned his need for love towards girls. The girls he liked sure did love the big grin on his face. When Benji turned sixteen, he met Lisa. Lisa was eighteen, and the best looking girl Benji had ever seen. Lisa's father was absent from her life as well.

Benji went on to share, "We talked for what seemed like hours about our lives. One night, we went to Lisa's house and she told me she was going to show me how to become a man. I had sex for the first time, and it was amazing!"

After that night, it became Benji's goal to love them and leave them, just like his dad did.

"Over the next twenty years, I was addicted to the feeling of new—new relationships, new women, and new jobs. When I turned thirty, I felt like something was missing from my life. I visited the little church in my neighborhood, and I found what I was missing. JESUS! The feeling overwhelmed me as I walked down the aisle and gave my life to Christ. It was amazing. While the experience was incredible, my personal life remained the same in some ways. I gave up drugs, alcohol, partying, and even the need for multiple women. Yet, with everything I surrendered, and even with my love for God, I am still unable to experience victory over needing new things."

He went on to share, "I've been married three times, I have five kids, and I have attended several churches. "New" always starts off great. In new relationships, I always feel like she is the woman I have looked for all of my life, but when the newness wears off, it is time for me to make a change. I love going to the hospital and holding my wife's hand when the baby is coming. I even stay around because of the feeling a new baby brings. But, once the newness wears off, I create drama so the relationship can end. I love going to new churches. When they announce me as a new member, everyone stands and claps with such excitement, but after a few months or years, it just gets old."

Benji's story may seem extreme, but it's a reality for many people. The people that come into Benji's life are just as frustrated because they continue to give him another chance hoping "this time" things will change. Benji's Expectation Level is 1. He's on the ground level. When you're a Level 1, it's hard to become a Level 8.

Benji's father did not stick around, so in our coaching sessions we did not find the root to the generational pattern. Many times it's very hard to break a generational cycle. In this case, Benji's only hope to shift the generational cycle is to become what he hoped for, rather than what he got from his father—instability.

In Chapter 3, I'll cover how to break generational patterns. I'll discuss in detail how to become what you hoped for, rather than responding to what you actually received.

BRENDA: EXPECTATION LEVEL 4

I chose to share Brenda's story because she not only reached Level 4, but she also defied a lot of the stereotypes I witnessed over many years of ministering and counseling people.

I have always looked at "the haves" and "the have nots." The "haves" are embellished with beauty, money, talents, and friends. They have the life everyone wants.

Then, I met the Smith family. I was preaching in their city at an awesome church. Brother Smith was an incredible teacher, leader of the men's ministry, and an associate to the pastor of the church.

Brenda Smith, his wife, was the whole package. She was beautiful, and she had an amazing voice that moved the congregation to worship God. She had a nice car, beautiful children, a very good job, and she was loved by her Sunday school class. On the surface, one would think their family had it all.

That Sunday, I remember having a heavy anointing on me, and I noticed Brenda was very moved by the power of God. The closer I got to her, the more I noticed that her heart was heavy, and she was broken under the power of God. I called my wife to come forward, and we proceeded to minister to her.

I leaned forward and said quietly in her ear, "God is releasing the pain you are carrying from your father."

She broke, and the cute little lady started to sob; she knelt and called out to God. After service I asked the pastor's permission to talk to her and her husband. I later learned she had multiple affairs on her husband, and she was in trouble with child protective services for the abuse of her children. Needless to say, her personal life was in shambles. Like always, I waited 24 hours before talking to Brenda and her husband, to ensure we were not dealing with the anointing but real life!

As we sat down to talk, I asked, "Will you tell me about your father?"

Strangely, her husband grew very emotional, and she reached out and held his hand. I thought right there, "Oh no! Tony Hall, what kind of mess did you get yourself into?"

Without a lot of emotion, Brenda started sharing a moment from her childhood.

"I was twelve years old, my mother told me God had opened so many doors for her, and she was being used by God to touch churches in our state."

Brenda recalled the excitement on her mother's face. In her 12 year old mind, her mother's words were a really big deal.

She continued, "At the time, I was happy for my mom. She told me I had to help with my brother and sister, and take care of my father when he got in from work."

Brenda recounted that her mother felt like she was "a big girl, and she was going to be used in the ministry alongside her."

After Brenda's mom left, her father would come into her room and remind her that it was her responsibility to take care of him. He started touching her, which soon led to sexual relations with his 12 year old daughter. While he sexually abused her, he also verbally abused her, and called her names. She told us she tried harder to please her father, but things only got worse.

"I was confused because during the day, he was the greatest father in the world, but at night, the monster came out," she said.

I was so outraged!

"Why didn't you tell your mother?"

What she said next blew my mind.

"Each time I tried to tell her what was happening, my mother would stop me and remind her that "little girls that lie go to hell." I knew my mother would never lie to me, so I endured it; we never talked about it again."

At thirty something she was abusing her kids, having multiple affairs, and she was left wondering where God was in all of the mess.

My wife and I left to pray. We needed to try to absorb the situation before we could start helping the family navigate their difficulties. After two days of praying and seeking God, I scheduled another meeting with Brenda and her family.

After we sat down, I asked Brenda some important questions.

"Where is the relationship with your dad now?"

"It's very difficult to look at him because of the love and respect our little church has for him and my mom."

I told her in order for us to stay involved we must come up with an action plan, so she could be healed. I advised Brenda to sit down with her husband, her mom, and her dad.

It was almost as if I asked her to curse God and die. She started making excuses (like most abused people do). After three months, she called her mother and reached out to me to schedule an appointment with her family. Her father went into a rage. He had a massive heart attack, and he died shortly thereafter.

The next six months were filled with accusations, rejection, and denial from her mother about this "Godly man."

I later came back into the area and wanted to see how things were going. She told me what happened, and shared that her father's death did not bring them closer to each other.

Her mother loved my ministry, so I invited her to have lunch with me and my wife. As we talked about ministry, I asked her to be my special guest that night during service. She honorably agreed, and said she would be there.

As we continued to talk, I asked her, "What is your assignment from God these days?"

"I'm assigned to preach deliverance and set the captive free."

She walked right into the trap. She hung herself with her own words. It's amazing that we can have a burden for others, yet we are cold and careless when our family is lost and broken.

That night after service, we sat down with Brenda, her husband, and her mother. I asked her mother to repeat her assignment from God.

She repeated with pride the same confession she told me earlier, "to preach deliverance and set the captive free."

"What about starting with your daughter?"

After the shock left her face, I asked, "Where were you when your daughter was being sexually abused by your husband?"

I asked Brenda to tell her story. Her mother was sick to her stomach and almost passed out listening to the gory details.

Her mother was broken, and she apologized as Brenda told her story.

She started, "I was molested by my brothers when I was a little girl. I worked a few meaningless jobs to stay away from the abuse of my brother. Eventually, I got a job cleaning a big house in the area, so I lived there most of the time. When I was 17 years old, I met your father during a revival at church."

Turning towards Brenda, she said, "He was my ticket out of my mother's house and being abused by my brothers. On the night of our wedding, I felt like I had to confess I was scared to have sex with him because of the abuse I suffered. Your father told me he should have never married me and would someday find a virgin to have normal sex with him. Our relationship was cold and dirty. I always felt like he was never really present during our intimate moments together. The church told me that I had to stay until God changed your father. Like my mother, I needed an escape, so ministry became my escape. I stayed away most of the time hoping he would find some other woman to fulfill what he needed. I'm horrified to know you were that woman."

After much repentance and a lot of counseling, Brenda is living a victorious life in Christ. She still struggles with her relationships with her children, and she is trying not to hide in ministry and church work. Rather, she is choosing to go home and work on her relationships with her husband and children.

However, I'm sad to say, her mother continues to live in denial. Rather than growing as a grandmother, she goes from church to church, trying to find acceptance. She does not have a solid relationship with her daughters, her sons, or her grandchildren.

I asked Brenda if she had forgiven her mother, she said, "I realized my mother was a victim; the woman who I believed was the most anointed and powerful woman of God, was hurting too."

DERRICK: EXPECTATION LEVEL 6

Looking on the surface, you would think Derrick had it made as a man and leader in his church. I was almost embarrassed to ask him the question I asked most men and women when I sit down to talk to them.

"Will you tell me about your father?"

Like many others I've asked the question to, Derrick lowered his head, looked back at me, and said, "My father was absent; he was a womanizer, a drug abuser, and he was never present for his kids."

After counseling people for more than thirty years, I must admit I was confused. Most people with this story end up with a bad marriage, become a drug abuser, and commit adultery.

I sat up in my seat and asked Derrick, "How did you become who you are?"

Derrick told me about his earliest memory of his father. "My dad was self-consumed and never seemed to love anyone but himself. When I was younger, I would see him going in and out of the homes of women in our neighborhood. I mean, he didn't even hide it from my mom; he was just out of control."

Derrick spent the next thirty minutes sharing how he remembered his father physically abusing his mother. Yet each time, he recalled his mother begging his father not to leave them again.

Looking at the great man Derrick had become, I wanted to understand how he overcame the things he witnessed as a child. "How did you overcome the pain of your childhood without repeating the dysfunction?"

Derrick said, "You are assuming I never repeated these behaviors because you know me now, but when I was a young married father of three, I did some of the same things I watched my father do. When I turned 30, I was on the brink of divorce, my kids hated me, and I felt lost and alone. I totally surrendered my life to the Lord Jesus Christ. Even after receiving Christ, I still had the scars of my father. Everything I was doing was normal behavior for me; I didn't know any better."

As I continued to listen to Derrick's heart, he went on to say, "One tragic day I got a call telling me that my father was in the hospital, and he was not expected to make it through the night. I must admit, I went to the hospital to spit on him before he went to hell. Yet, when I got there, no one was there to hold his hand or visit. The doctor came into the room and gave my father the news, and I felt compassion towards him. I just stayed. I even did something I never thought I'd do, I laid my hands on him like I would any other broken man. After I heard myself praying for my father, I broke down and wept. I just stayed with him. The frail man I called father reached out his hand, made contact with my face, and wiped away the tears. His hands were smelly and hard, but it was the hand of my father."

"What was your reaction?"

"Well, after standing there in shock, I cried out to God and asked Him to give my father some more time. The doctors said he wouldn't make it overnight, but God heard me and gave my father five more days. I was the only one who visited, and I never left his bedside. He was in and out of consciousness, but I was able to ask him the hard questions. My father told me he was sexually abused when he was a small child, and he said he was physically abused by his father because he was sexually confused as a teen. He told me the only thing that quieted his pain was alcohol, giving him a false sense of boldness. He even told me when I was born he was so messed up he would feel aroused when he changed my diaper, and rather than giving into the pain, he left."

Derrick told me the next five days were filled with stories he wouldn't have known, had he not stayed in the hospital.

"On the last day of his life, my father sat up in the bed, and asked me to forgive him. He rested his hands on my head, prayed that God would be good to me, and released the little boy within to be free. My father didn't know the Lord, but I felt something in my body I've never felt. For a moment, I felt like my father would get up, put on his clothes, and ask me to take him home. After his simple prayer, he leaned over, kissed me on my cheek, fell back, and died. I can't tell you how I felt. Here I was 45 years old, and I'd missed all that time with my father. I'm thankful God gave me five days. The reason I'm a Level 6 on your expectation scale is because I purposed my mind that I would not become my hurting father. Rather than being angry, I have accepted and understand that **fathers hurt too.**"

Derrick faced a decision that most people who reach Level 6 face. He discovered he must live with 360 degrees of revelation. 360 degrees of revelation occurs when one has the capacity to understand where they've come from; they understand the other person's perspective, and they understand how to handle both viewpoints. People with 360 degrees of revelation work diligently to ensure they do not repeat the mistakes of others. They walk in freedom, while also working to heal the people they hurt also. Reaching this level takes maturity.

Benji, Brenda, and Derrick each saw their life experiences from a different angles. Each one legitimately felt the pain of not having a healthy relationship with their father. Yet, because they are different, I served them differently. Love is a guiding force, but my approach is not the same for everyone.

A person's Expectation Level helps me serve them better. So, if I'm asked about a situation or a problem, I use my years of experience and my passion for life, but I also use their Expectation Level. If they are a lower number, my expectation is very little.

I wish I had this type of wisdom when my father was alive. He was a miserable person, and often used his words and actions to belittle the people around him, including me. Now that I am older and wiser, I realize how I could have managed my expectations differently, thus creating an opportunity for us to work towards a more functional relationship. For over thirty-five years of ministry, I've spent countless hours loving people who struggle with all kinds of problems and unfavorable life experiences. From fatherless sons, to people battling racial prejudices,

I've had an opportunity to hear people's stories, but after getting to know them and loving them with little to no expectation, we became friends. I've been able to engage in their world and establish a meaningful relationship with them because at my core, I realize everyone has a story. Whether they were molested, struggled with abandonment issues, or battled mental, or emotional problems, God gave me wisdom and showed me how to minister to people I didn't even know. However, I've often wondered why I couldn't minister to the man I knew and loved—my father.

As children, most of us live our lives believing our fathers have the power to do any and all things. I remember the way my father would "wheel and deal" with people. He would drive fast and cause loud outbursts of laughter to erupt from each of us. He cooked better than most women, and he organized things like a pro. He was trusted by his employer and loved by his customers (they would give him the keys to their home). My father was honored by his family, and he was a great leader for many of the families in Georgia. Yet, despite all of the honor and respect my father experienced, he was hurting.

When a father is hurting, someone often pays the penalty for the hurt and pain.

DISCOVER YOUR FATHER'S STORY

I want you to look at your father differently. I'm not asking you to forget the hurt and pain your father caused you to endure. I'm asking you to discover his story before you allow more days, months, and possibly years to go by.

Death has a way of stealing the future from you. Don't allow death to take the opportunity to understand away from you. If I had known what I know now, maybe I would have sat down with my father, with NO expectations. The tragic loss of his wife, and the responsibility of living with seven children was a weight my father could not bear. All of the pain started to rise to the top when he became paralyzed. He was forced to retire. I now believe he was not equipped to give me love. My father's inability to love me had nothing to do with me. His loving me was not because I wasn't good enough, or because I wasn't a good father, husband, preacher, or son. He couldn't celebrate my success because he was a broken man. I'm at fault because I wanted him to become to me what he couldn't become.

The last time I talked to my father is not my fondest memory. He lived in Detroit, Michigan, and I lived in Houston, Texas.

I will never forget the day because I rented a limo to take my wife and friends to the Taste of Texas Steakhouse. On the way back from dinner, my father called. He told me he wanted all of my siblings to come home and paint the basement. Well, I lived in Texas, my oldest brother Ronald lived in Arizona, my younger brother Brian lived in Washington State, and my sister, Marcia, and my baby brother Barry lived in Tulsa, Oklahoma. I knew rallying all of us from different parts of the country was unlikely. Trying to help, I told my father I would call my brother Derrick, who also lived in Detroit, and have him call a painter to do whatever he needed.

When I made this suggestion, my father exploded and started to curse me out. I was so shocked and taken back by his response. When he finished putting me down as a man and preacher, I told him he would never hurt me again. I just hung up the phone.

My emotions were everywhere. The pain I felt when I received a call two days later telling me my father died, is unimaginable. I think he knew he was dying, but he couldn't bring himself to call his children together to say goodbye.

Today, I live with the regret of not being able to share some things with him without expectations.

Because I missed the opportunity to talk to my father with no expectations, I'd like to share my thoughts with you. The decision to investigate and discover your father's story could be the key to rewriting your story together. Discovering his story is not a ploy to ignore or discredit the hurt and disappointment the relationship has caused, but it could be the gateway to healing.

I have a friend named Pastor Mike Cox. His dad was the most incredible man and father that I had ever met. He loved me like I was his son, and I felt his love.

Perhaps some of you have great fathers like Pastor Mike, but for those like me, discover your father's story. Ask God for the wisdom to find peace in your life, and understand that fathers hurt too.

MY PRAYER OVER YOU TODAY:

Father, as my brothers and sisters uncover their father's story, I pray you give them wisdom for the next steps. I pray they release the hurt they feel, and they have the courage to walk in the freedom their father never experienced. I pray for peace in their lives and the lives of their children, in Jesus' name, Amen.

CHAPTER 2

PAIN OR POISON: IT'S YOUR CHOICE

Everyone, in this life, will experience pain. I wish someone would have explained that truth to me when I was 7 years old sitting in front of my mother's casket. All of the adults in my family were grieving, and there were no words for their own pain, so they couldn't offer any explanation for mine.

MAUVE CASKETS AND SHINY CARS

I still recall the day of my mother's funeral. It was cold that morning. The limos were sitting in front of our house waiting for my family to get into the cars. A mauve casket was nestled in the front car. At the time, I didn't understand that my mom was inside. I was just excited about riding to church in the shiny car.

Little did I know, this would be the last time I would see the woman who made me feel like I was the only person who mattered in the world. Although I felt like this treatment was exclusive to me, the truth is, she loved all of my siblings this way.

From time to time she would ask, "Anthony, do you want to stay home with mama today?"

Of course I would say, "Yes ma'am!" with great enthusiasm.

At the time, I didn't know she made up excuses to my dad so I could stay home with her during the day. I felt like she was a supermom, and I loved loving her. She could make you laugh when you behaved, and rip your behind if you acted in a manner that was unacceptable. I loved my mother, and I still miss her.

That cold morning, after not seeing her for 3 weeks, I was going to church to say my final goodbye. I stood in line with my family because there were so many people. As we waited, I was clueless. I had no idea the beautiful mauve casket at the end of line held my mom, and she would make her final procession on this earth.

She was not going to kiss me on the cheek and tell me things would be alright. When I saw her in the casket, I was overwhelmed with emotion. I kept asking, "Why? Why? Why?"

My uncle said, "Tony, never ask God why." This was my first encounter with a person telling me how to approach God. I had questions, and my 7 year old heart needed answers. The day of my mother's funeral was bigger than the mauve casket, and the shiny car. It was heartbreaking and painful. This was the day life changed for me in so many ways.

"SOME" PEOPLE

After the funeral, I spent the next thirty-five years thinking there must have been something I could have done to save my mother. The thought weighed heavily on me. It was hard growing up seeing other children with their mothers, laughing, and loving.

In my heart, I was thinking, *if God is so good, why did I have to lose my mother?*

Because I never fully understood the truth about pain, I believed a lie. I believed some people had it made, and life for them was easy. I didn't think I was a part of "some" people. I regretfully admit I made my family endure so much pressure during major holidays and birthdays.

I know my thoughts may sound crazy, but I used to think white people who lived in the affluent neighborhoods, had attractive physical features, had thin frames, and lots of money, were able to escape hurt and pain.

My good friend, Pastor Mike Cox, helped to dismantle this lie in my life.

One day he looked at me and said, "Tony, everybody has some pain, and nobody has it made in this life."

It took me several years to really absorb his words, but he was right. Keep in mind I experienced the trauma of losing my mother at the tender age of seven. At that age, there were some things I didn't have the mental capacity to understand. I needed someone to help me process my pain in a healthy way.

Everyone has a degree of pain they have experienced, currently experiencing, or will experience in life. When I understood this truth, it allowed me to get through the next season of pain without getting stuck.

I say a season of pain because pain occurs when we go through something. It could be a result of our own actions, or it could be the result of someone else's actions. In a season of pain, I believe we determine how long the season will last, and the impact it will have on the people around us.

Some people, in their season buckle down and accept the pain. They make the people in their lives suffer endlessly. Those people typically end up bitter, and all of the relationships around them are destroyed. Others go through their seasons of pain with the help of God. They use their experience to touch someone who has gone through, or someone currently going through a similar situation. Let's take for example one of the many things that happened to me; I have been able to use my pain to help so many people.

A NEW FAMILY

By age fifteen my life was stained by drugs, alcohol, poor grades, and fighting. I loved to fight, but I was no good at winning. I simply loved the attention I received, and I experienced a sense of belonging as a gang member.

But, I remember my brother-in-law, Willie Davis, invited me to a musical at his church. Although Friday nights were a standing party night for me, he mentioned the prettiest girls would be at church that night; I decided to clear my calendar. I'd never been to a Pentecostal church before, I just wanted to see the girls.

When I got to church that night, I'd never experienced people so passionate about praising God. My brother-in- law was telling the truth. The girls there were beautiful. I came dressed to impress. I wore lime green pants, a shirt that belled at the bottom, and I sprayed my hair with Afro-Sheen before walking out of the door. I looked a hot mess!

With conviction, Darlene Davis started singing, "I must tell Jesus all of my trials, I cannot bear these burdens alone." For the first time, I heard the message in the song, and I saw the condition of my life without God. I began to cry. My heart was gripped in that moment, and I ended up at the altar. That evening, March 28, 1973, I gave my life to Christ. My life has completely transformed since that day. I felt so good about my decision and my transformation, but everyone around me was not as excited— including my father and fellow gang members.

I've endured times of great tests and trials. They were all attempts to get me to turn back to the lifestyle I left behind. It's been forty-three years, and I'm still a follower of Jesus Christ.

I tell people it is the best mess I have ever been inside. Because I experienced rejection from my father and family for wanting to live for God, I became adopted into the family of God. Church became a safe place for me. I wish I could say I was a perfect example of a young Christian. My life was resurrected, and I came out the grave, but taking off the grave clothes took a while longer.

UNLAWFUL TOUCHES

My pastor noticed me and started to invite me out for lunch, sometimes dinner. As a 15 year old new believer, I thought I must be very special. I felt loved by my pastor. One day while riding in his truck, he reached over and asked me how it felt when he put his hands on my thighs. I pushed his hands off of me. I told him it felt horrible, and I would appreciate if he never touched me like that again.

He laughed it off and said, "I was just playing with you, you need to lighten up."

After I got home, I thought to myself, "Come on Tony, this is your pastor. He loves you; you are taking this the wrong way."

Several weeks later, his wife was in the hospital. She was in bad shape. When we went to see her, the thoughts of my mother came back over me. It was hard to see our first lady cough up blood. It was painful for me to watch. After we left the hospital, he said he needed to get something from the church, and he would take me home afterwards.

When we got to the church, I stayed in the front area, thinking about his wife. I kneeled at the altar, asking God to touch our first lady and heal her. After getting up and going back to the front of the building, he called me into his office. When I got back to his office, he had his shirt off, and he was lying on the couch. He asked me to get some lotion and put some on his back. I was shocked because my pastor was asking me to rub his back. I put a little lotion on my hands and reluctantly reached for his back. When I touched his back, he whipped around and grabbed me in my genital area. I was shocked beyond belief. I pushed his hands off me and threatened to kill him if he ever touched me like that again.

Like I said before, I came out the grave, but those gave clothes were still on me.

When I threatened him, he looked shocked and grabbed his shirt. While riding home, he reminded me that he was the only one who cared about me, and he only wanted me to feel loved.

I called my sister and the family who was close to me to tell them what happened. At 15 years old, I didn't have filters, but I knew my pastor's actions were wrong.

No one believed me, which made matters worse. The pastor was able to turn the church against me, and they treated me like an outcast. Then, things were very different from things today. Today, abuse is broadcast in the news; then, it was hidden and folks continued having church.

I finally left that church when I got married, and I moved away from Detroit with my young family. The church was bursting with members. They owned the whole block, and had some of the most amazing musicians in Detroit. After I left in 1979, the news surfaced that I was not the only young boy who experienced our pastor's unlawful touches. People started leaving in droves, but no one, including my sister, ever apologized for not helping me during my trial.

GOD CAN USE YOUR PAIN

The question becomes, "What do I do with the pain?"

Most people would have left the church forever. It's likely they would have hated the people in the ministry and recruited others to do the same. Although I was young, and not the man I am today, I knew God could use my pain to change lives forever.

During your season of pain there is a small window of time for you to determine what you will do with your pain. One of my all-time favorite scriptures is 2 Corinthians 1:3-5:

> *All praise to the God and Father of our Master, Jesus the Messiah! Father of all mercy! God of all healing counsel! He comes alongside us when we go through hard times, and before you know it, he brings us alongside someone else who is going through hard times so that we can be there for that person just as God was there for us. We have plenty of hard times that come from following the Messiah, but no more so than the good times of his healing comfort—we get a full measure of that, too (The Message).*

When I was young, I did experience a season where I tried to make sure nobody ever got that advantage again. So at the first sign of abuse, I got out in a hurry. The problem with escaping is that I missed a lot of what God wanted to do in my life by running away from the pain.

A lot of us run from situations, but God is using those situations to teach us some lessons. These lessons grow our faith, and we cannot stop until we experience every lesson designed for us. I believe some of our trials are tailor-made in order to fulfill our destiny. I do not believe another person could have gone through what I went through because God knew what He was calling me to, and He knew the people I would minister to in the future.

If you are going to become successful, you'll want to come to terms with the notion that God did not send the pain. However, He allowed it to happen, and He will use it to allow you to reach others.

CHOOSING PAIN OVER POISON

It's been forty-nine years since my mom's death, but I still remember her. I have fond, loving memories of her, but certain times of the year were (and still are) very hard for me. Holidays are times for family and sharing, and most people look forward to those times. I didn't look forward to the holidays.

As a young, married man, I was so depressed on my mom's birthday, my birthday, Mother's day, and Christmas. Unfortunately, my family did not look forward to those days either because they knew I would be in a funk. Everyone walked around on eggshells, hoping I wouldn't blow a gasket. I was unaware of the pain I was causing.

The pattern was the same. The day before was great. The day after was great, but on those specific days, I sabotaged the experience for my family because of my pain. My pain became the poison that infected everything around me.

I will never forget the gift I received on my 40th birthday after a conversation with my Aunt Ernestine. She sat me down and told me some truths about my mom, and it was as if I finally woke up. After having a come to Jesus meeting with my aunt, I sat by myself, talked to God, and apologized to my family for causing so much heartache during those days. I received healing through 2 Corinthians 1:3-5. I then used my pain and the Word of God to help others, who had no parents, heal.

Because I received that revelation, I am now the spiritual father to people all over the world. It gives me great satisfaction to have men and women honor me as someone they lost, or never had.

It's easy to look at people who have what you wish you had, and feel some bitterness or envy. However, it brings me so much joy to meet this need in others.

Take note of what I said. I had to heal my pain first. So many people look for money, men, women, church activities, or even other things, to heal their pain, and the consequences are not rewarding. Remember, it's our responsibility not to allow our pain to slip into poison.

IT'S YOUR CHOICE

I know I'm sharing with millions of people who experienced mental, verbal, or sexual abuse. The reason I know it is based on my personal experiences. Abuse from a father, a mother, a teacher, or a pastor, is wrong.

While I was abused, I did not mention the pastor's name or church, partly because he is dead, and his name will not change what occurred. Further, it is not my intent to hurt anyone by sharing my story.

After the incident with my pastor, I was shocked at his ability to turn a good number of people against me by saying that I was a liar, or that I took things the wrong way. Whatever you want to call it, NO ONE should grab your private parts, or be stretched out on a table in their office with their shirt off. Calling his behavior inappropriate would be an understatement.

His denial was so strong, I started believing I must have been crazy. I and I started believing the people who said I should let it go and put it in the hands of the Lord.

However, I understood years later if God was going to use me, I needed a plan to not allow the pain to turn into poison.

Thirty years after the abuse I went back to Detroit when my mother-in-law was dying from cancer. While sitting at her bedside, I felt the Lord speak to me. He told me He was not finished dealing with the abuse from my pastor. Taking God at His word, I arranged a time to speak with my pastor. I didn't know what I would say to him, but I knew it was finally time to deal with the past.

When I walked into his office, rather than feeling infuriated, I felt sad for him. After some small talk, I told him I wanted to apologize for the pain I felt towards him all those years. He never once apologized for his actions that night.

He said, "If I did anything to hurt you, I want to apologize."

Shocking myself, I got down on my knees, and asked him to pray for me. He put his hand on my shoulder and prayed a prayer. I got up, hugged him, and left totally free. My apology was not for him, but it was totally for me. After hearing he died, I can truly say I have no unfinished business with him.

I remember when I was about 28 years old, at a revival in Houston, Texas, I felt a strong urge to call people to the altar who had been sexually abused in their lives. As I was saying it, I felt a spirit of fear come over me. When I called out to pray for people who had this experience, not one person moved.

I wanted to run and hide. I heard Satan say, "You fool, now you have made a total clown of yourself; you didn't hear from God on the matter."

When I didn't see anyone come forward, for the first time, I talked about the abuse I experienced. The church was full, and I started to hear people wail and travail.

At the end of my testimony, I said, "since no one experienced abuse but me, I would like the pastor to pray for me."

Before I could turn around and ask for prayer, fifty people started coming down the aisles towards me to get prayer for their situations. The anointing to pray for sexually abused people started that night, and it continues to flow everywhere I travel. The largest altar call to date has been in the Philippines, where there were approximately seven hundred women and men who shared the same experience. My wife and I laid hands on all of them, and we felt chains break off their lives.

I learned from that experience that as I prayed for the abused, I received my own healing from abuse.

What are you suffering from? You have the key in your hand.

Will you unlock your pain and find the purpose of your pain on the other side?

Or, will you unleash the poison on all of those around you?

Are you ready to receive healing? Are you ready to experience freedom?

As you share what God has delivered you from, it can turn into passion, and those who hear you can be healed. It is possible.

As crazy as this request may sound, I now ask God to always allow me to remain acquainted with the feeling of the pain I went through because if I forget, I fear I won't have the compassion for others who have experienced hurt and pain.

MY PRAYER OVER YOU TODAY:

Father, like so many others reading this chapter, I know the pain of abuse. Help my brothers and sisters understand that you feel what we feel. Allow them to know, you are here to help them in their time of need. I pray from this day forward, they will experience your healing touch. As they are healed, I pray they will remember the grace they received when helping someone else experience healing. I thank you Lord that we will not turn our pain into poison. In Jesus' name I pray, Amen.

CHAPTER 3
EVERYTHING IS SEASONAL

Everything in life is seasonal. This is another lesson I would have appreciated my father teaching me. I am 56 years old, and I feel as if I've lived five lives. My first life, was my life as a child. It was short. From the time I was born until I was 9 years old, there were good times coupled with very low times. I was too young to understand how bad things were, but the death of my mother left a young, fragile kid like me always feeling alone. During that time, I was introduced to beer, wine, weed, and porn.

My second life started when I was 9 years old, and it lasted until I was 14 years old. I started using drugs and alcohol. Life seemed more manageable when I was drinking, or smoking weed. I was comfortable, and I felt like I was in control. I started fighting in school and formed an allegiance with a gang. My father beat and punished me, but nothing helped.

My brother said we all needed counseling, but in the 60's and 70's, counseling did not appear as the most viable option for African Americans, as many did not see the value in it.

My father used to say, "All you need is a good 'ole butt whipping."

Believe me, I had a lot of those.

My 15th birthday started the next season of my life. As I mentioned in Chapter 2, I was invited to church to meet the pretty girls, but I ended up meeting Jesus. That night, I received Christ as my Savior, so I went home differently. The next three years of my life were highlighted by poor choices and major decisions. I dropped out of high school, my girlfriend became pregnant, and we decided to get married.

After getting married, I moved into the next season of my life. I could continue to share the seasons I've experienced, but eventually I feel like I got it right. I didn't pass every test, but I learned that life transitions seasonally.

TO EVERYTHING THERE IS A SEASON

Ecclesiastes 3:1 confirms this truth, "To everything there is a season, and a time for every matter or purpose under heaven." This scripture speaks to so much of my life. I've learned from my mistakes, and I have survived most of my storms. I've lived with the scars, and I live with the fortitude and grace to tell the world my story.

You can determine if you've embraced the truth of this scripture by your willingness to share with others how seasons in your life have ended. I'm not saying that everyone has to share their story openly, but when you have experienced the hurt and pain that I have, many people have a tendency to become jaded. They often want to climb into a shell to protect their sanity.

It's easy to hide behind your pain, but it's more fruitful to try, and make sense of it. At some point we will all be faced with that decision—hiding or facing our pain. We will either choose to find the lesson from our experiences, and use those lessons for our personal growth and development, or we will become bitter and refuse to move forward.

The greatest lesson I have learned is everything has a season, every trial has a shelf life, and no matter where you are today, if you survive and learn from it, things will change. Sometimes life gets better, and sometimes life gets worse. The determining factor for whether life gets better or worse lives solely in what you believe. Do you believe things will change? Or, do you believe things will remain the same?

I preached a series on wisdom, and in the series I talked about the seasons of life. I've been able to champion some of the greatest tragedies and not become bitter because I believe most things in life are seasonal.

There are three major seasons we likely experience, but if you stay the course, refuse to give up, soak in all of the lessons the season has to offer, you will experience peace and contentment with living. You'll also be prepared to minister to people for the rest of your life.

Let's journey through three areas that exist and mature in seasons: life, marriage, and sex.

1. LIFE

As a child, I talked all the time. I got so many whippings as a child because I wouldn't shut up. My father would visit the school every Tuesday, and the teachers would brag on my two little brothers. My brothers were very attentive and the teachers gave them rave reviews.

When my father asked about me, my teachers would bow their heads and say, "Mr. Hall, Anthony just won't stay in his seat, and he will not shut his mouth."

My father did not believe in "time-out" as a form of punishment. In those days, my dad made me find my own switch, and he would tear up my backside. As a result, I was pretty good Wednesday, but by Thursday, I was right back to my antics—yap, yap, yap.

I said so much as a child, people would likely think I wouldn't want to talk anymore. Yet, I've been privileged to preach all over the world to various cultures, and in every type of church.

I learned to embrace my gift. Now, when I minister to people rather than encouraging them to change who they are, I try to inspire them to use their unique traits to fulfill their purpose.

I hate to admit this point, but my father taught us how to cook as boys out of fear. Because my mother died, and my father was left to raise young children alone, my father wanted me and my siblings to be able to cook, should our wives die and leave us with small children. He wanted us to be able to survive, so I needed to be able to do more than talk. I also learned to cook because in my opinion, my stepmother was a horrible cook. My siblings never complained, and even today they say I was stupid for hating her food; rather than complaining, I learned how to cook for myself. My siblings called me stupid, but my barbeque has made thousands of dollars, people have even inquired about me opening a restaurant. I took what I hated, and I allowed it to work in my favor.

2. MARRIAGE

I wish I would have learned that marriage is a seasonal experience. I can imagine many are ready to throw rocks at me for that statement, but truthfully, I've been with the same woman for thirty-eight years. When I first married her, I was a dumb 19 year old kid, thinking marriage was about having guilt-free sex.

I remember Denise being pregnant. In my mind, we were on our way to a life filled with happiness, but in reality, it was a life filled with happiness, tests, and trials. The reason I say marriage is seasonal is because we had a chance to build our lives on the good, bad, and everything in between. However, I believe the vows we take are a clear indication of the things we will experience during our season of marriage.

I remember very little about our 20's and 30's, but I do recall the time being filled with great pain. My wife Denise, on the other hand, remembers some great times. I wish I would have known we wouldn't be in our 20's and 30's always. If I had developed that wisdom, I would have handled some things differently.

In every stage of our lives, we tried to make the best out of situations. I believe it's been the love we have for God that has kept us through the years. It's easy to concentrate on what went wrong, but it's more powerful to concentrate on and help others understand what we did right. Because my wife and I have history with each other, we have the ability to touch so many others with our lives.

MEN BUILD, WOMEN RAISE

One of the many lessons I learned through the season of marriage is that God gives every man the ability to build his own woman, and He gives every woman the ability to raise her man. Here's the premise, God brought everything to Adam to see what he would call it. Whatever Adam called it, that's what it became.

In Ephesians 5:25-27, Paul writes, "For husbands, this means love your wives, just as Christ loved the church. He gave up his life for her to make her holy and clean, washed by the cleansing of God's word. He did this to present her to himself as a glorious church without a spot or wrinkle or any other blemish. Instead, she will be holy and without fault." After teaching this truth for twenty years, I determined that whatever I wanted in my bride, I could look to Jesus who is the author and finisher to understand how He built His bride.

First, Jesus loved His bride. His love was so great, He was willing to give His life for His bride. Jesus didn't wait for his bride to get it together. No, He loved His bride, the church, although we were bound by sin. So, I learned to love Denise in good and bad times.

Jesus loved His bride so much that when she experiences His love, she worships Him because of the love He shows. Then Jesus washed her with water by the Word of God. We all know the Word of God is consistent, so even when we are fickle and crazy, He uses the same word to chastise and love us.

When times were tough, Denise and I didn't like each other, but I would apply the same principle. I would tell her she is the ONLY woman I have ever loved. I would tell her how beautiful she is, and that there isn't another woman as beautiful.

I would pour it on thick. I told her she has made it impossible for any other woman to have me because of the incredible way she loves me. Jesus' reason for loving His bride the way He does is because He's going to present to Himself a glorious church.

I CALL HER QUEEN

Lastly, Jesus calls the church what it will become. I took heed to His method, and started to refer to Denise as Queen. I have called her Queen so long, people often believe it's her name. When I first started calling her Queen, she was embarrassed, but I have consistently called her Queen for twenty years, and she carries herself like a queen.

When we sit down with people we don't know, she is so gracious and kind. I don't know one person who doesn't like her. I believe her esteem is from my consistency in building her with my words and actions. She is not envious of other women. Remember, Jesus gave every man the ability to build his own wife. Today, we are more in love than ever, and I believe our actions show our love. People have stopped us in airports and commended us on how powerful the display of our love is.

Someone once said "It's all fake. There's nobody who can love another person that deeply for that many years."

I argue their point is not true because it is the way Denise raised her man. I hear people talk about low self-esteem. In my early days I wish I had low self-esteem because at least I would have had self-esteem. Denise Hall's husband had NO self-esteem.

The reason we worship Christ and lift Him up is because He loves His bride, and He aims to fulfill the desires of His bride. Denise was able to look past the dysfunction, the anger, and the rage at times, and she started to build up what I could become, and I have become that man. I am the man I am today because my wife made me feel and know I could become more.

Most men who are trying to become someone important, fight insecurities, low self-esteem, lack of support, and a world that has the ability to make one who dropped of school, got his girlfriend pregnant, and bounced from job to job feel success is impossible.

Denise encouraged and consistently reminded me that the ability to move the world was within me. Men are wired to love, praise, and honor. I do not mean the worship we give God, but every real man loves when his woman lifts him up.

Dear sisters, tearing your man down will not yield good results. Disrespect will shut out his ability to build on who you are designed to become.

3. SEX

I wish my father would have taught me about sex. I wasn't the popular kid, and I did not have a lot of sexual relationships. I'm thankful I didn't experience many of these relationships, not because of the moral aspect, but I'm positive I probably wouldn't enjoy my wife like I do now. I can't tell you the amount of men and women who are in their 40's, and they do not enjoy having sex. Sadly, they were never taught that sex is seasonal, and some were taught, but they didn't heed to good counsel.

Here's a thought to consider, God didn't make our bodies to misuse our organs and emotions so young. I'm not trying to preach to you, because I have made lots of mistakes in my life. However, I know if you are reckless with your sexual life, you will go into your later years and lose interest sexually. I read a report that suggested sex for those in their 70's is incredible. I almost got out of my car and started shouting, because I believe sex goes from something you do for your own pleasure to something you do to please the person you love with all of your heart and soul. When I was in my 30's and 40's, we had sex frequently. Today, in my late 50's, sex means more than just getting.

I want to encourage you to first build the heart relationship with the person you love. Build it in such a way that you can't imagine your life without them. When you do, you will survive the seasons of life because you understand everything is not about sex. Rather, everything is about the person you are married to.

LOVING HER HEART AND MIND

I had a class with a group of young men in their 30's. The topic of sex came up for me to address. Most of them talked about how they are not happy because of the lack of sex they were experiencing.

I told them if they learned how to love the mind and heart of their woman, her organs wouldn't have a problem desiring them. I explained to them that if they didn't learn how to love her mind and heart in about fifteen to twenty years they would likely face a monster that had the ability to destroy their marriages, menopause!

They sat with blank stares because they had not thought beyond the current moment. I told them the reason my wife and I are so happy in our sex life is a result of me building equity in her through the years.

When she started to experience some of the seasons women face, we were able to thrive. I never thought about going outside my marriage to take care of my personal needs. Now that we are on the other side of menopause, life and sex are incredible!

Years ago, we conducted a marriage seminar in New York. We split the class by gender, and Denise and I taught the opposite sex.

In my class, there were about fifty women. During my time with the ladies, we spoke about sex, but one lady had simply had enough of me telling them what their husbands needed. Rather than putting her question on paper anonymously, she interrupted me to tell me she's not interested in sex with her husband.

I had to address her statement publically, because it felt like she dared me to tackle "that statement" whole group.

I asked her, "What do you think the problem is, and when did this feeling start?"

She said, "I'm 37 years old, and all my husband wants is sex. Things have been this way since I accepted Jesus."

It's possible she wanted to curse me out for my response.

I said, "Your husband was made to want sex, and rather than being mad at him, you ought to be mad at God. God gave men that drive. To have an attitude with him is wrong. Secondly, your husband is young, and he's yet to learn how to make love to your heart and mind, and you are not helping him by having the attitude that he's a freak for wanting sex all the time."

She looked confused by my comments.

"Just because you received salvation that does not mean your private parts got saved!"

Her problems were many but in this case, she didn't have balance in her life. I didn't want to appear mean or heartless, but this young lady didn't know what she was going to experience in the next ten to fifteen years would make her wish her husband would desire her all the time.

I believe too many Christians have a false sense of life. Too many of us think once we get saved, we lose the responsibility of being good mothers, fathers, parents, lovers, friends, and good employees.

I believe Christians should be the greatest mothers, fathers, employees, and yes, the best lovers in the world. Both men and women go through changes every ten years or so, and it will be helpful on so many levels if we would accept that sex is seasonal.

Life doesn't seem fair all the time. Marriage takes work and intention. Your sex life doesn't have to become boring or non-existent. Everything exist in seasons.

Hold on, it won't be winter forever, spring, and summer are just around the corner—seasons change.

MY PRAYER OVER YOU TODAY:

Father, I pray my brothers and sisters will enjoy every season of their lives. Allow them to know every season has a time and purpose. As we come to the end of one season and move into another season, Father we ask you to help us to pull exactly what we need from that season, in order to make the next season even better. In Jesus' name, Amen.

CHAPTER 4

YOU CAN'T BEAT LIFE

"Be not deceived; God is not mocked: for whatsoever a man soweth, that shall he also reap."

~Galatians 6:7 NKJV

There are things I know now, that I wish I would have known then.

One of those lessons is that life keeps moving whether you're ready or not. The seasons of life come and go so quickly. Once you've traveled through the years, endured the tests, and learned some of the lessons, you find contentment in the golden years.

Most people view the golden years as a time to retire to the beaches of Hawaii. However, I believe you enter the golden years when you finally synchronize with the rhythms of life. In essence, you've learned to waltz through seasons with peace and grace. I'm living in my golden years. It's not that I have enough money to retire to the beach, but I have found a resting place within the rhythms of life, and I am at peace.

THE LESSON OF DOUBLE DUTCH

Have you ever watched children jump rope?

Double Dutch is my favorite. Double Dutch is played with two jump ropes turning in opposite directions. Two of the children stand outside the ropes, and they sway back and forth until they catch the rhythm of the ropes. They know it's important to wait until the right time to take the leap. If one goes in before the other, everything would be thrown off, and the game would start again. I've spent the last thirty-eight years of my life with Denise; during our time, there's been a lot of swaying back and forth.

Today, we understand the rhythm of life. Most of the time Denise is more discerning of the rhythm and she keeps me from jumping in too soon. We have raised three children, planted churches for thirty years, counseled hundreds of couples, been extremely poor, and we've had wealth. We've been accepted by some, rejected by others, hurt by pastors, bruised by denominations, lost and gained a lot friends. We've traveled all over the world and ministered to churches representing so many different cultures, and we still have our joy and peace. Before we enter any situation, we hold hands and sway, catching the rhythm before we jump.

DON'T LET LIFE MANAGE YOU

Finding the rhythm is one way you manage your life. When you find the rhythm, you can enter your golden years with peace, not regrets. While I have some regrets, thankfully I was young enough to have an opportunity to fix some of the mess I created in my younger, foolish years.

During this chapter, I hope you will be able to use my insight as a guide to help you fix what you can, and count the things you can't fix as power for the course.

People are generally dishonest; they ignore wisdom, and they live with the hope that they can beat life. Indeed, life will catch up with you.

Living free comes when we accept the fact that life really does happen in seasons.

Every ten years you will come face to face with major changes in your life. If you miss a season, or mess up a season, you will pay for it in another season. Most people either blame others or the devil for seasons they missed or messed up. It's easier to blame others, rather than taking responsibility—"It's me; I did those stupid things!"

I really believe the only reason I have been effective in my marriage, ministry, and parenthood is because I take responsibility for a lot of issues that I caused, either because of ignorance, immaturity, or thinking I could beat life.

You might ask, "How did you think you could beat life?"

I'll share an example. I know a lot of women who have sex with men, get pregnant, and find themselves living in a mess for the rest of their lives. Well, I had unprotected sex with my girlfriend many times, and it never occurred to me that the same situation could happen to me. I thought I could beat life and somehow avoid the consequences of my actions.

The look on my face when Denise said, "Tony, I'm pregnant!" I'm sure it was priceless.

There were so many thoughts that raced through my mind. I thought:

What will her dad say?

What will our pastor say?

What will my parents say?

How will a broke joker like me take care of a baby?

The difference maker for me was my father's teachings. He taught me responsibility. After Denise told me the life-changing news, I went home, pulled my mind up to start thinking like a man, and told myself I must marry this girl because it would be horrible to have a child, and not be a part of his or her life.

We got married, and we had two more children. I have worked tirelessly for thirty-eight years because of immature decisions. I know you may not want to own up to your mess, but if you are going to become effective, you must take ownership of the choices you made and deal with your decisions. You have to manage life, you can't allow life to manage you.

ALEX -THE LOVER

Alex was so smart, and he knew how to talk to women. He had a list of women who couldn't wait for him to call. Alex's father saw his son had so much potential and tried to warn him of such reckless behavior, but Alex was having too much fun.

Alex got one of his girlfriend's pregnant, and like other foolish men, he accused her of doing to him what he had a history of doing to lots of women.

Alex enjoyed the drama of her calling and begging him to stay in a relationship. Rather than being responsible, Alex moved to the next beautiful honey on his list of women. After the baby was born, the young lady believed Alex would man-up, and help take care of his daughter. Not Alex, he had too many women.

Alex was the young lady's first love, but he did not care. The young lady was so hurt and damaged. Eventually, she moved to California to get her life on track without Alex.

She went to school, received her degree, and joined the single parent's club.

Meanwhile, Alex continued to live his life. One night, Alex got drunk at a party, and slept with the neighborhood prostitute. It was almost like the prostitute planned to trap Alex, or perhaps Alex was reaping what he had sown.

The prostitute called Alex one month later; she told him she was pregnant. Alex was already paying child support to the mother of his daughter, and he didn't want to the responsibility of paying two women, so Alex married the prostitute.

She was a very loose and nasty woman, and she was looking for a man to take care of her. After having six abortions and suffering with a horrible disease, Alex found himself living his worst nightmare. She told Alex she lost the baby, but she was never pregnant.

Alex was hooked.

Some may wonder what happened to the first lady and baby who moved to California.

As time has it, the little girl grew up and wanted answers about her father's whereabouts. Alex's daughter finally found him, living with her two little brothers. His daughter was so hurt and bitter. She was old enough to express her feelings concerning what he did to her mother, as well as how she felt as a forgotten child.

Alex is older now, and his heart aches every day for the love of his daughter.

Do you see how the seasons you messed up find you, and demand payment for the previous season?

Alex left his first love and his daughter on the sidelines with no concern, and now, his daughter left him wanting and needing her love and attention. His reckless behavior has left him alone. He has no one to love him like his daughter.

My heart still breaks for Alex.

I have seen this scenario hundreds of times. Most of the time, the fathers and mothers who leave and abandon their children never have a moment of peace because they thought they could beat life.

MEET THE PARENTS

Preaching in Indianapolis, Indiana, the pastor asked me to go with him to visit the nursing home. He was an incredible evangelist, so I was honored he asked me to attend. When we arrived, I noticed everything was so fancy. It was obvious that only wealthy people lived in this nursing home. I also noticed there were no African American employees.

As I took in the beauty of the environment, a little, old man wheeled his wheelchair right into me. He begged me to talk to him. I didn't want to appear rude, so I stopped to talk to him. After I finished speaking with him, another lady approached me with the same request. I finally found myself in the room of a cute, little, old lady. She laughed at me because it almost seemed I was being tackled by the patients in the home.

We had prayer with her, and as we walked out, I hugged and laughed with as many of the people as I could. As we wrapped up our visit, I complained about children putting their parents in a nursing home and leaving them there without regard.

"God is going to judge their children for their actions," I said.

The evangelist I traveled with, put the car in park and said, "Brother Tony, I don't agree with your assessment of the nursing home. I've been in ministry for sixty years, and I really know a lot of these people. You mentioned a lot of their children are going to answer to God for forgetting their parents in the nursing home. Truthfully, a lot of those parents never thought they would get old. When their children were young, they were enjoying their lives, and their children weren't their priority. Most of them hired professionals to help raise their kids. Now they are old; their kids are enjoying their own lives, and they have hired professionals to take care of their parents."

They thought they could beat life, and now life was beating them.

I do believe in forgiveness and grace. As a matter of fact, I believe I'm somewhat of a poster child for the grace of God.

Dear friend, please understand, your decisions have consequences, but forgiveness is available for our sins and dumb decisions.

MY PRAYER OVER YOU TODAY:

Father, I personally know grace and forgiveness are available for bad decisions. Therefore, I am asking you to help my brothers and sisters know a better day is coming. I would never ask for you to take away the pain from bad decisions, but I ask that you give them wisdom to go through and endure the season. Lord, their lives will be used to help others deal with the consequences of their poor decisions. Thank you for total victory, in Jesus' name, Amen.

CHAPTER 5

BECOME WHAT YOU DESIRE

One of the greatest challenges I've encountered while writing this book is reaching inside my heart and asking myself the hard questions, the questions I normally ask other people...

Why are you so selfish?

Why does success carry the weight that it does in your life?

When you grow up with no self-esteem you have a tendency to look at things through the lens of suspicion. Oddly, I have great love and compassion for others when they are wading the waters of their mistakes and poor choices, but when I messed up, I immediately pounced on myself. Truthfully, it was a horrible way to live. When I analyzed the root cause of my actions, I discovered a layer of wisdom that helped me navigate those feelings.

THE TRUTH

Here's the truth, we are fallen people, and our fallen nature ignites our need for Christ.

Yes, we need to accept Christ in order to go to heaven, but most of our issues take root because we cannot beat life. Romans 3:23 reads, "For everyone has sinned; we all fall short of God's glorious standard."

Because of this truth, we should be kind and consider others in light of our failings. Often, we are very unforgiving of our sins, shortcomings, and failings in others. Meaning, we hold others to a standard we do not meet.

I've learned over time it's easier to own what has happened to you.

There are so many people who do not own their failures, which is why so many people live miserably. However, when we take charge of our lives, we become stronger.

It's impossible to live up to this truth if you don't think much of yourself. Likewise, it's impossible to live with this truth if you think too highly of yourself. Living this truth requires that you be honest with yourself. This truth has helped me develop a healthy value of myself.

I'm always in the middle of the road because I know myself. I remember my past, and I know God knows me intimately, which explains why I have mercy on people.

Mercy flows out of me because I consider myself. I know some Christians who are so hard and stringent, but they are hiding their issues. They likely hate themselves so much for their struggles, they transfer their hate onto other Christians because they see themselves in others.

We all have things we are not proud to admit. The struggle can be intense at times, and finding an exit seems impossible.

I can remember people telling me to pull myself up by my bootstraps, but in my mind I always asked, with a dumb confused look, "What on earth does that mean?"

I wanted to get up, but I felt I didn't have boots or straps.

A FATHER'S REJECTION

My father was my hero, but the more I craved his acceptance, the more rejection I felt. It didn't matter how motivated I was by my accomplishments, he always found a way to splash cold water on my excitement.

I recall times in my early teenage years, when I'd come home smelling like weed and alcohol. My father would sit, shaking his head, announcing, "Everyone I know named Anthony is nothing but trouble."

His words were piercing and hurtful. Today, I hardly ever use my name when expressing my identity. I'm sure he did not know a lot of people named Anthony, but hearing those words come from my father penetrated my being. His words made me feel like, I should have another name, and if I did, I would be better in life.

I eventually understood my name had no bearing on my poor choices; being without Christ, living without Him, gave my actions no standard.

I gave Jesus my life March 28, 1973. I'll never forget that day. I beamed with joy. The Holy Spirit was radiant and shining bright in my heart, and I'd never felt so good. I didn't have a desire for drugs, alcohol, or hanging out with my friends. I only wanted to run home, and share with my hero that I finally made a great decision—I decided to follow Jesus.

With tears flowing down my face, I shared my testimony with my father. Something powerful happened to me and I knew it.

He looked up from reading his newspaper, and said "It's just a fad, and it will end soon!"

I was devastated, and I cried myself to sleep that night. My father didn't have to get up and rejoice, but at the lowest level, I was hoping he said, "That's great son!"

For the next two years, whenever my father was upset with me, he punished me by not allowing me to attend church. Truthfully, he was upset with me because I chose to attend a Pentecostal church. When I turned 26, he shared that he and my mother had dreams of me and my brothers becoming Baptist preachers.

Living in that type of environment was devastating.

When I felt discouraged, Satan would say, "Get back at your father. Go back to using drugs. He doesn't care."

I did not allow that voice to form my decisions; my actions would not hurt my father. My actions would have hurt me; ultimately causing me to pay the price.

I remained true to the Lord.

REMEMBER WHEN...

One of my spiritual sons had trouble in his marriage. During that time, I gained wisdom that allowed me to consider myself and my journey. I found myself so critical when I was giving him counsel.

I did not want to seem harsh. As a matter of fact, I thought I was helping him. When he called with good news, I found the negative, and strongly pointed it out to him. At the time, we were just friends, but God used David to help me grow.

One night after talking to David, I felt a strong conviction from the Lord. The Lord pointed out to me that I wasn't listening to David. I was making him pay for what my father did to me, and it was not fair. I was shocked and truly convicted.

Today, no matter what he shares with me, I always tell him he's a great man, and I'm proud of him and his accomplishments.

In the earlier stages of our relationship, I did not know his father was an abusive alcoholic, and my words were trauma to an open wound. After drastically changing my attitude, he gave me the greatest honor a man can give to another man. He became my spiritual son. He's only five years my junior, but he respects and honors me like my own children.

I often tell David he is the one individual who helped me grow up, and become a spiritual father to hundreds of men and women throughout the world.

Pastor David Johnson's life taught me to listen to people with affirming ears, and if I have to give them bold counsel, I start and finish it with love and praise.

Perhaps you are making others pay for your brokenness.

Maybe your children are hurting because you are making them pay for your mother or father's choices.

Some are making pastors pay the price for their parents. It's very hard to benefit from a man or woman's ministry when you are trying to get them to be something you missed. It's time for you to repent to them and start being to them what you desire, rather than what you received.

Stop to remember, and choose a different course of action. When you start being what you desire to the people in your life, you will become a better parent, a better lover, a better friend, and a better member.

LEADING WHILE BROKEN IS A DISASTER

I believe the people who pay the greatest price for our brokenness is our family.

Sometimes I'm overwhelmed by the love of my wife and children. Because I married so young, I've often felt I was a troubled kid trying to raise kids. I had the stepmother from hell, and a very bitter father. I'm sure my family suffered greatly.

I believe my son felt the brunt of hurt from having a broken, young, foolish, and ignorant father. Simply put, I was mean, frustrated all the time, and I didn't know how to love. My dear, sweet wife knew how to pray, and she made me feel like being great was possible.

When my son turned 7 years old, not only was I his father, I was also his pastor. I remember buying a set of drums, and I screamed at him until he played them to my liking. Sometimes my family grew quiet until they'd observed my mood.

If I said something funny, everything within my children and wife lit up with joy. Of course the times presented a very different outcome. I'm still so sad about my actions during that season.

Thankfully, I was able to keep my family because my core was whole. I had a deep love for God and a deep love for my family. However, my life was consumed by brokenness.

When you use drugs, drop out of school, get your girlfriend pregnant, get married young, and move 1,600 miles away from home, things can be very hard. My love for God kept my family together.

My son's family didn't have the same story. A divorce caused his family to fall apart.

We finally had an opportunity to sit and discuss the things happening in his life. I had no idea my son was handling so much at the time. My son told me the divorce was bad, but the worst part of getting divorced was telling me. I nearly fainted.

Teaching people all over the world how to stay married for life, yet my son's home was falling apart. I was not shocked because my son didn't want to tell me, I was shocked because my son thought if he told me I'd go into Clarence Hall mode and start condemning him.

While I could not fully understand the pain my son felt from his divorce, I told him I could share wisdom I've gained to help him get up and move forward. I also reminded him of my love for him. The things I shared were things he needed to hear from me—his father, his hero, and his pastor.

I told him he would be able to minister to people I would never be able to minister to because he had an experience I've never encountered.

I stepped out of my world, and placed myself inside his world. While he shared his concerns with me as a son, husband, and father, I listened and felt sympathetic towards his heart. Things shifted for my son when I was transparent. I told him I would want someone to talk to if I were going through the trial he faced.

His transparency, and my ability to listen without judgment afforded us the opportunity to have a better relationship. I am so grateful for that opportunity because I really am honored to be Anthony Q. Hall Jr.'s father.

MY PRAYER OVER YOU TODAY:

Father, I pray for people who have endured life experiences that left them hurt and broken. Lord, heal their hearts. I pray my brothers and sisters have the wisdom to become to others what they wished they'd received. In doing so, the people in their lives will have an opportunity to experience your grace and compassion. In Jesus' name, Amen.

CHAPTER 6

EVERYONE HAS A STORY

When the numbers in your age move from single digits to double digits, you're in the big league, or so I thought.

There was something empowering and exciting about having the word "teen" associated with my age. Things were different. I wasn't a young kid anymore. My father and stepmother were finally buying me "big kid" items for Christmas.

At 13 years old, I remember telling my little brothers, "I feel almost grown!"

Truthfully, some things actually changed. I was exposed to more things. My body changed, and I started noticing things I had not noticed before my teenage years.

I remember the peach fuzz growing on my face, and I used a hairbrush to brush both hairs. My Adam's apple was more visible, and my voice register was lower (you couldn't tell me I didn't sound like Barry White).

The signs of maturation were evident in my voice and body, but mentally, I hadn't changed one bit. I was still young and foolish. I still used drugs, and I fought in school. I even dismissed the things my parents taught me. I was still a boy.

I HAD A STORY

From the outside, one likely assumed I was a lost case.

However, I had a story and purpose to fulfill.

Some people wrote me off as a troubled teenager bound for destruction, but God never gave up on me. The overcoming chapter of my story exists because deep down, I have always had a deep love for God, and I wanted what He wanted for me.

While I battled life, I really loved the Lord, and I was willing to hang on to Him because no one believed in me. I've now learned to appreciate the beauty of this time in my life. I don't owe anyone anything. God brought me out. He fought my battles with anger and no self-esteem.

Having Jesus as your anchor is the key to understanding the value of your life. I hated myself most of my marriage, so it was impossible to show complete love to my wife and children. If my love for God was not strong, it's possible I would have never learned how to love. God taught me how to love.

SEEING THROUGH THEIR LENS

Everyone has a different perspective, and a different lens in which they view the world.

The more you try to force people to see life through your lens, the more frustrated you will become.

Years ago, I thought my wife's glasses made her look so cute and sexy. I remember saying to her, "I wish I could wear glasses."

Her glasses made her look smarter, and I thought if I had glasses, I would be smarter.

One day, she looked at me and said, "Honey, I promise you don't want to wear glasses. It's a pain."

I couldn't really process her words because I had great vision.

Fast forward thirty years, and needless to say, I am tired of these glasses. My vision is great when I wear my glasses, but I can't see anything when I'm not wearing them because the lenses hold the correct prescription for my eyes. They work just right for me, and help with my vision.

When I counsel people, I always start by asking questions to understand how the person sees life, marriage, ministry, or whatever topic we are going to discuss. Based on their view of things, coupled with facts about their story, I formulate a counseling plan.

When I talk to counselors and they are burned out, I know the reason is directly linked to the facts surrounding the other person's story, and the counselor's interpretation and response to it. The counseling session will not be effective if it's based solely on the way the counselor views things, as opposed to the way the person being counseled views things.

Take eyeglasses for example, two people can have identical frames, but if they try on the other person's glasses, they will immediately find both have different lenses.

I find that I am more effective when I find out how another person sees things. I not only develop my counseling plan according to their needs, I also direct my prayers for them on their vision.

LET ME GO

While visiting a sweet lady dying of cancer, I was moved by her courage to transition peacefully. At the same time, I watched as her family made every attempt to abort her decision. They made her feel guilty about dying because of their pain and selfishness. I'm not judging them, but she wanted to die peacefully. She was ready to go, but they weren't ready to let her go.

Each time the family entered the room, they would say "Auntie, you must confess Jesus has healed you! Don't let doubt overtake you; keep believing."

I remained quiet, and I prayed silently as they cried and wept.

Here was a lady struggling to help her family cope, but feeling she had fought as long as she could.

As her pastor, I'm sure she contemplated whether or not I was disappointed and viewed her decision as a lack of faith.

After everyone left, I went back into the room.

"What do you want me to pray?" I asked.

She stared at me, although puzzled and confused. She didn't know what to say.

"I will agree with you. Matthew 18:19 reads, "I also tell you this: If two of you agree here on earth concerning anything you ask, my Father in heaven will do it for you. What do you want me to pray?"

She said "Pastor, on one hand I want to go to heaven, but so many of my children are in trouble."

"I understand. God is waiting on us to agree, and I believe He will answer our prayers."

The little mother grabbed my hand and said, "Pastor, I'm ready to go home with Jesus."

I took off my shoes and coat, and my wife and I climbed up into her bed. We sang songs of praise with her; she could only move her mouth. Moments later, she drifted into a coma. By the next morning, she slipped out of this world, and into the arms of Jesus!

When I consider this family and the woman battling cancer, there's no one to blame.

They both saw things through different lens. The family thought if they prayed more their mother would get up and be able to go home—things would go back to normal.

On the other hand, the lady had fought as much as she could, and she had no more strength to fight.

While I understood both perspectives, it was my job to agree with the lady's heart. I believe she saw a glimpse of Jesus, and His light made the world looked darker and darker.

She chose to leave this earth to live with Jesus.

I know that many of you would argue me down if this were your family, but you must understand that God gives each of us a set of lenses, a perspective, and we will make decisions based on what we see.

When I talk to people as a life coach, I spend most of the first conversation discussing an eye examination, and I help them based on how they see themselves and their story. The confessions below help me to see my life more clearly. Feel free to confess them over your life.

MY CONFESSIONS:

Who I was, I am no more. I have changed.

My mistakes do not complete my story.

I am not finished until my destiny is complete.

My story is not over until there is a happy ending.

MY PRAYER OVER YOU TODAY:

Father, so many men and women struggle with their life and their story. Their story should not make them ashamed because it has the power to glorify your mighty works. Help them to see things differently, and as a result of their new vision, change what they say they believe. I pray they understand their story will bring glory and honor to you in the end, in Jesus' name, Amen.

CHAPTER 7

IT'S NOT YOUR FAULT, BUT IT IS YOUR PROBLEM

Society has created a huge space for victims. Many people live with the harsh realities of their past and the brokenness that comes along with it. As a coach and counselor, it's hard to watch people live in that space. They can't seem to move beyond their hurt. They are stuck in their pain, and they let their pain prevent them from getting to the place they are destined to go.

LIFE HAPPENS TO US ALL

Life happens to all of us. I have worked with all types of people, and in my thirty-six years of ministry, I have never met a person who has not been impacted by life. Whether abuse, abandonment, the death of a parent, divorce, or some other life circumstance, there is an impact.

Life's tragedies aren't planned. You can't protect yourself from the pain of an unexpected death of a loved one, or the decision of a parent to choose to ignore his/her responsibilities.

In helping people, I have settled on the fact that I'm no better or worse than the people I help. Life has happened to me too. However, I have figured out how to cope and deal with the aftermath of my circumstances in a healthy way, and I use my understanding as leverage.

Even in reading the Bible, it's clear that life happens to some of the best people. We sometimes have the tendency to only pull out the scriptures that make us happy or push us towards hope, but life happened to the greatest men throughout scripture.

As much as I love to read the Psalms of David, I wouldn't want to live his story.

My father could have taught me this lesson well.

In Chapter 1, I shared at length some of the horrible things that my father encountered in his life, but I never saw him become a victim.

My brother has mentioned that he heard our father moan from time to time. He recalls my father saying "I didn't sign up to raise all these kids."

Yet, he stepped up to the plate, and did the best he could with the hand he was dealt.

I remember the night after my mother's funeral clearly. Her siblings called a meeting to discuss what should happen with the "younger ones"—meaning, my brother Barry, Brian, and me.

My father came into the living room, thanked everyone for their support, and told them they did not need to plan because he promised my mom he would never separate us.

Indeed, he kept his word.

My father could have sent us to live with other family members, but he honored the commitment he made to my mother.

It was not a perfect situation, because times were hard. But, my father chose to take responsibility for his life and his family, despite the drastic turn of events he experienced.

Many of the people I minister to today don't stand up to the problems that come with living. I think it's important to add that my father never professed his love for God. He did send us to church, but I never remember him confessing his reliance on God. He made a decision to confront his problems directly.

TAKE CHARGE OF YOUR SITUATION

I'm familiar with this lesson also. Some things simply weren't my fault, but they became my problem. I had to make a decision. I went through a lot of pain and suffering, but I never chose to quit. I got my girlfriend pregnant at 18 years old, married her, and with no education, we had three children. Yet we made a vow to God and one another.

It amazes me how so many people that knew us then, are attempting to take credit for the success we have experienced. Truthfully, no one thought we would become the people we are today.

Denise and I wanted to prove our lives were not a mistake. Thankfully, God has made a great impact in our lives, and He has allowed us to impact others.

For this reason, I truly encourage people to make their life great. The goal is not to impress others; rather, it is to give God praise.

USING OUR EXPERIENCE TO HELP OTHERS

I met Jerrod in San Antonio, Texas.

Jerrod is a young man I've recently connected with through his wife. Jerrod's wife remembered the messages I preached a while ago. After preparing to visit a divorce attorney, she stood in the shower and cried out to God because she was not at peace with her decision. Her appointment was in two hours. As she cried out to God, the Lord impressed on her a message that I preached in 2002 entitled, "At The Point of Can't Take No More, but Not in Distress!"

She remembered point by point, and reached out to my wife and me on Facebook®. She wanted us to pray over her life, and she asked us to call her because the matter was urgent.

Truthfully, I didn't remember her, but she reminded me of the woman pleading before the unjust judge. She needed a miracle, and she was not going to stop until she heard my voice.

My wife and I were out of town, and I normally don't check messages while I'm resting, but her consistency in trying to reach me stood out. My wife gave me permission to reach out to her and we connected for about ten minutes. She told me about her decision. However, she said she remembered the sermon I preached, and she would do whatever I told her to do.

Wow! I didn't remember her, but God knew both of us.

Because we were out resting, I wasn't doing much praying and seeking God, but the urgency in her voice connected with my spirit, and within minutes, I received a word from the Lord on her behalf.

I told her it was the will of God for me to connect with her husband, and that God was going to do a miracle in their lives.

That evening, to my surprise, Jerrod called me and wanted to talk.

What did I ask Jerrod?

You are correct!

"Jerrod, will you tell me about your father?"

"My father was a good man. He worked all the time, but he never had time to speak into my life. I remember getting home from school one day, I was about 16 years old at the time, and I noticed a U-Haul truck in the front yard. I was so excited because I thought he purchased our family some new furniture. To my surprise, my mother pulled me aside to tell me she was leaving, and she said I couldn't go with her."

You see, because his father worked all the time, his mom was his everything.

I could only imagine what came to Jerrod's mind as he saw his anchor ride away in the U-Haul that day. He didn't see his mother again until he was 28 years old.

Twelve years can be an eternity for a child without the person who taught him everything about life and love—all the things great mothers teach their children.

Jerrod's father didn't realize his mother left until he returned home from a long day's work. I'm sure his father knew it, but nobody thought it was important enough to tell young Jerrod the truth.

While his father dealt with the tragedy, he had with no compassion towards his son. His actions pointed Jerrod to the streets for love and acceptance. He started drinking heavily, and partying, to fill the hole he felt in his life from his mother's abandonment and father's lack of emotional support.

When Jerrod turned 20 years old, he met Candace. He and Candace fell in love quickly, and before they knew it, she was pregnant. Because Jerrod didn't really have a mother to tell him how to handle things, and his father lived on his job, Jerrod chose the lesser of two evils. He went to work, and never spent time with Candace.

He was taught this behavior from his father's actions. After Candace had the baby, she and Jerrod decided to move in together to have a happy home with their new baby girl. As soon as they moved in together, Jerrod quickly realized sleeping with a girl, and taking responsibility for a girl are two very different things.

Jerrod told me they fought every day, and there was no peace in their home. Candace couldn't understand why Jerrod was so mad all the time, so she made up her mind that she was going to leave just as soon as they got their income tax check.

On their way home from a family outing, she broke the news to Jerrod. In a fit of rage, Jerrod started screaming at her and didn't see the man fixing a flat on the side of the freeway. Jerrod struck the man, and killed him instantly.

As he sat in court, he constantly looked around to see if anyone had come to testify on his behalf. On the day of sentencing, his father showed up late, and told the jury he loves his son, but his son needs to control his anger.

The judge asked Jerrod to stand, and gave him twelve years to life sentence for taking another man's life in a fit of rage.

Jerrod was distraught. When he looked around the courtroom, no one was there to blow a kiss, or to even cry on his behalf.

GOD WILL SEND HELP

By the time I got the phone call from Jerrod's wife (of one year), Jerrod was a lost man. He was an alcoholic; he had one child from his first girlfriend Candace, another child with his wife, and her three kids from other relationships.

While I have never been to jail or killed anyone, so much of Jerrod's story resonates with me because I understand loss. Although some of the things that transpired in his life were not his fault, all of it was his problem.

I personally believe our connection became a blessing because Jerrod was so low, and he needed an intervention. After speaking with Jerrod, I gave him some homework to see if he was really ready.

The reason I give homework is because most people just want someone to make them feel good about their dysfunctional lifestyle, and it allows me to better understand their Expectation Level.

My goal is not for those I counsel to just feel better, I truly want them to be better. I want them to experience wholeness and live the abundant life Jesus made possible.

Having a person like me in your life can, at times, taste like the castor oil we all avoided as kids. It tastes like death in a bottle, but if you can swallow it and allow it to work, it really is "good for what's ailing you," as my mom would say.

I gave Jerrod one day to decide if he was willing to accept my help, stop drinking, stay away from bad influences, and be totally honest with me.

I gave him one day to decide because I wanted him to see the benefit of a new, functional life. I could not allow him to see me as the problem, so I gave him a little time to decide.

By the next day, my phone rang and on the other end was a man, totally sober, rested, and ready to take on Tony Hall from North Carolina.

Over the next hour and a half we talked about every aspect of his life. After explaining story after story after story to me, I showed him compassion and love.

The one thing that helped Jerrod was doing his homework with me. Twice a day he had to quote these words, "A lot of what I went through was not my fault, but it is my problem."

I told Jerrod if things were going to change, he needed to do the following:

- Forgive his father and mother. They probably did what they taught was best. It's not his job to figure them out; it's his job to forgive them

- Forgive the mother of his daughter. Before she left him, he had already left her.

When I raised this point, Jerrod said, "My body was there sometimes, but my actions were not there. I can't do anything about my daughter not having me for 12 years, but I pray that when she finally finds me, I will be a man that can give her the love that she deserves."

I went on to say:

- Never drink again. You cannot change your life by medicating yourself with any kind of substance that impairs your mind.

- Become what you wish you had rather than responding to what has happened to you.

- Tear out the rearview mirror, more accidents happen when people are looking behind, so concentrate on the great things before you.

- Accept that some things that happened were not your fault, but they are your problem to fix. Commit to spending the rest of your life, if need be, fixing the things you have destroyed.

- Make a vow to God and your spouse that you will help others that may be struggling in the areas you have overcome.

Jerrod is choosing to do the work every day. He's choosing to take responsibility for the condition of his life. He's preparing for a better future. You can too.

Denise and I are humbled to love and minister to people, and each time God brings someone into our lives, the light comes on and we see our past reflection and what we could have become.

In those moments, we choose to extend the grace, love, and forgiveness that Jesus gave to us.

I know some people are still hiding in the cave of what happened to them, but my prayer is that this chapter will open the cave, and they walk out and never go back to the bondage again.

You see, when you refuse to get out of the hurt, bondage, and pain, you take the weapons from your abuser and continue the abuse they started in your life. A better life is possible.

MY PRAYER OVER YOU TODAY:

Father, I ask that you set my brother and sister free from the pain and bondage their lives have given them. When born, they inherited the dysfunction of their family, and the dysfunction has continued for years. Give them the courage to confront their problems and take responsibility for their life. I speak life over them, and I believe they will walk in freedom, and live the overcoming life you planned for them before time began, in Jesus' name, Amen.

CHAPTER 8

THE TRUTH ABOUT ME

Honestly, I never get tired of reading about what Jesus thinks about me, or how he loves me. The Bible consistently affirms and clarifies the Lord's thoughts concerning me.

In this chapter, I'll introduce my children to you, and encourage you to freely express how you feel about the people who matter most to you.

One of the things that saddens me deeply is that my father died without telling me what he thought of me. I believe he loved me, but he never said, "Tony, you are a good preacher, a good father, a good son, or a good man."

Because I didn't receive his affirmation, I have only visited the place where he is buried once. The graveyard is such a sad, lonely place if things are not dealt with properly.

In 2000, I recall going to the graveyard to tell my father I had to release the pain, hurt, and negative words he spoke over me as a child and man.

Once I completed that mission, I've never had a desire to return.

My dad was my hero, but he couldn't bring himself to say anything good.

I'm sure some of you wish your father would have told you how he felt about you.

I realize now that the affirming words of a father have the power to change as life evolves. When I think about how God feels about me, my interpretation and appreciation for His words changes also.

For example, Psalms 23, when I was in my twenties, thirties, and forties, that scripture had different meanings to me. The way I applied the scripture to my life was likely different at twenty than thirty simply because I really didn't understand the flow of life in order to make better decisions. Because of my misunderstanding, I still lived with some guilt because I didn't know how to become a better husband, father, and preacher.

Now, in my fifties, the scripture has an entirely new meaning every day because I realize every decision I make affects everyone in my life.

Whether it's taking better care of my body, how I interact with my wife, engage with adult children, or working with the people I get to pastor, it ultimately affects everyone in my life.

I also realize my legacy is on the line. I see so many pastors and older men who were loved because of their actions. Then, all of a sudden, one decision destroys their name forever; it's so sad!

Therefore, I want my children to know exactly what they mean to me. Now that Denise and I have finished raising them, we contribute to their lives as a voice of reason and wisdom. I believe the value of these words will be evident in their lives now and increase when I have gone home to live with the Lord.

As I thought about this subject, I don't remember one thing my grandfather said about anything, so this book is dedicated to my grandchildren, Tre and Danyella Hall, Andrew, Jacob, and Jaden Bramwell, and the grandchildren to come.

DARRELL D. ALEXANDER

When I came into your life, I was a young, 18 year old child with no direction. Your mother and I got married as an attempt to fix the mistake we made in disobeying God. Although you've suffered many things, I'm so proud of you, and I'm so grateful you have another chance at doing some great things. When I talk to you now, I'm excited that you took the lemons you received, and are making lemonade.

As a father, I pray you will always know that you are an overcomer. God's hand is upon you, and I believe you will touch many people with your powerful testimony. I was touched during our last conversation. You said, "You do know that I love you, don't you?"

You heard me half-heartedly answer, and you came right back and asked, "Do you know that I love you?"

Through everything we have been through, you still honor me as your father. When I think of everything I have done in my life, to hear my oldest son remind me of how great I am spoke volumes to me, and your words made me glad I didn't let go and walk away. Your mom and I think you are a great man of God, and one of these days, we will see you proclaiming the word of God. I speak blessings on your wife, kids, and grandkids.

ANTHONY Q. HALL JR.

My son Anthony is a great man of God.

Anthony, I say you are a great man because I know you have gone through some of the hardest times in life, yet you continue to get up and work to make things right.

Once in a conversation, I told you that if you used your pain to help people, you will be a greater father than me, and you will be able to help people I could not help.

The second reason I believe you are a great man is because you were born when your mother and I were young, troubled, and didn't know what the heck we were doing.

I was a young father, and I wasn't a good one. I wasn't fathered well.

Just as you fight the demons of your father, I fought with the demons of my father. The difference is, I realized I had issues and struggles, but with the help of God I was able to overcome them.

Anthony, you are a great man because you didn't use my failures as the reason for your problems. I was terrified thinking of how you'd turn out.

During your teen years, I worried about the man you were becoming, and I'm sure my father shouldered the same fear concerning me. Yet, God brought you out with His mighty hand, coupled with many prayers from us and people who knew us.

Things changed the day we were in Cracker Barrel. We sat at that the table and with humility and honor, you shared some things I didn't do right.

While you acknowledged me as your hero, you also felt that in order for us to move forward, I needed to understand how I hurt you as a man and son. That day changed my life because I did the same thing with my father. He chose to throw my feelings back at me, and things were never settled.

Thank you for allowing me to repent to you. Our relationship is stronger than it's ever been. That day at the restaurant, I saw the man I raised, and I am proud of you. I've watched you on your job "wheel and deal" with your customers, and it brings me such joy.

You are an amazing young man, and the son of my glory. I have never been as smart as you when it comes to fixing things. You just have a knack for it.

You are coming into wisdom, and it is amazing to see your life unfold.

I love and appreciate the way you love me, and the way you share the nuggets of wisdom you use in your personal life. I know you are going through some tough times, but I have full confidence that you are going to rise above it. I'm so grateful you carry my name; because of you, my name, Anthony Q. Hall Sr. will never fade.

FELICIA CAMILLE BRAMWELL

Felicia, you were the child born to bring happiness to our lives. We were young, far away from home in San Antonio, Texas, and I felt totally sad and discouraged. When you were born, you were the first daughter in the Hall family, and you brought so much happiness to your young parents.

It may seem like too much pressure on a young baby to do that, but it's the truth.

One day while holding you in the room at Methodist Hospital, I held you close and began to sing, "You are my sunshine, my only sunshine, you make me happy when clouds are gray. You'll never knew dear, how much I love you; please don't take my sunshine away."

Truly, you were and are my sunshine. You always knew how to make me smile, and you have grown up to become an incredible mother to my grandsons. My desire is that you use your life to touch people for Jesus. I have noticed since you got married, you have always tried to share with people the wisdom you got from your parents. I know that one day, your wisdom will catch up with your age, and you will be powerful for the Lord Jesus Christ.

I have always been proud that you wanted a man who had qualities like me. One of the greatest honors a father can have is to know his daughter(s) want a man like him. Your choice lets me know I did right by you, and that I was a great example of a father and man of God.

Never stop being who you are. You have the call of God on your life, and the world will be greatly blessed because of you, my sweet daughter, Felicia C. Hall Bramwell.

APRIL NICHOLE HALL

April, you have been so close to your father's heart.

Once, a lady came up to me and said she knew that you were my favorite.

I was shocked at her opinion, because I love you, your brothers, and your sister the same.

Truthfully, I think she made this observation because we have so much in common.

First of all, neither one of us were planned and shouldn't have been born, but we are here by the grace of God. Second, we both had hard lives and nothing came easy for us. I know all four of you had tough lives, but you have come through it with a deep love for God, and the willingness to love people, and minister to them.

Your first ministry was to your parents, and I am so grateful for your support.

As a little girl, you always had the ability to make my heart feel that everything would be alright. I can't speak for other fathers, but of all the kind and nice words we have received from those we have ministered to, it blesses me to know my baby is my biggest cheerleader.

I have witnessed so many men and women move thousands of people, but lack the respect of their children. I am so grateful for your love and respect.

You never had it easy. I remember the day the doctor walked in and told me "Sir, somebody is going to die today."

It was May 10, 1982. He said, "It's going to be the baby, the mother, or both of them."

I can't tell you how numb I became after hearing those horrible words. I was only 24 years old, and I didn't comprehend, but I knew I couldn't lose my wife, or the precious child. I knew you both had to live to prove them all wrong. They sent several people to talk some sense into my stubborn brain, but I made a vow to God that you would give your ministry to Him and I stood on the promise I made to God.

I remember you telling me several times, it's not fair how your sister can get away with things and you cannot, but it was because of the vow I made to God.

You have now become a woman who will touch nations for God, and I know so many people have already been blessed by your amazing life. People often wonder why I cry like a baby when you sing, but when I see you, I see a miracle.

You are your father's little girl. Whomever I give you to as a wife must know he is marrying a true woman of God.

April, I will always love you, and I cannot wait to see the incredible things you are going to do for Jesus!

THE BLESSING OF SPIRITUAL FATHERHOOD

I have never built a mega church, but I have touched hundreds of men, women, and children. When I leave this world, I will have birthed many spiritual sons and daughters, and I give God all of the praise.

This conception was not a natural one, rather, it was born out of the need for affirmation, love, acceptance, and covering. These types of relationships were not planned, but each connection was made by the Spirit of God. I have a spiritual connection with my sons and daughters.

There is no way I can say everything I'd like to say to all of my spiritual sons and daughters, but I want to express my love to a few of you. Please know, my love is equally expressed to all of you.

Pastor David Johnson, you are the one person who has taught me how to become a loving spiritual father. From all the different challenges we faced, I'm thankful you didn't allow me to quit when I wanted to give up on everything. You saw something in me that I did not see at the time.

I remember once we had a blowout argument. After a few days of not speaking, you called me and left a message that said, "Only you can destroy the relationship we built, but you are not going to be the one who causes it."

After listening to your message, I called you, and we patched up our hurting relationship. From that day until now, we have repaired our relationship, with the help of the Lord. Today, we have an incredible relationship. You still call me to check in, or you ask for advice only a father can give.

What's powerful about our relationship is that you are also my best friend, and we are closer than any of my brothers. Thank you, on behalf of all of my spiritual sons and daughters. From you, I learned what they may need, and all the credit belongs to you.

I always tell you, "I know if anything were to happen to me, you will be there to ensure mama and my kids are okay."

You are an amazing man, and a great son!

MY PRAYER OVER YOU TODAY:

Father, I pray all my sons and daughters will see themselves as my children and spiritual children. Let them know the love I have for them is real. Allow them to know they can come to this chapter at times when they need to know the love of a father, in Jesus' name, I pray, Amen.

CHAPTER 9

THE SECOND GREATEST GIFT

"He that finds a (true) wife finds a good thing and obtains favor from the Lord." ~Proverbs 18:22 (NASB)

For some lessons, my father could not be my teacher. Here's another lesson he couldn't teach me: the second greatest gift given to man is his wife.

After my mother died, my father never quite found himself, although he remarried four years later.

He later told me he married his second wife because I needed a mother.

That conversation went totally wrong.

I really believe my father never knew the favor he found in my mom because he never received Christ as his personal Savior. It's only when you have love for God that you fully understand the favor that comes with having a good wife.

I wasn't taught that lesson, yet I feel uniquely qualified to teach this lesson to my sons and daughters. My sons need to learn how to treat their wives, and my daughters must learn to wait on God to send a man who loves and celebrates them.

GOOD TO YOU VS. GOOD FOR YOU

I want every son to know your wife is looking for you. As men, the problem we face when we are younger is that we are just too dumb to know the difference between what feels good to us versus what is good for us. Her eyes, her legs, her hips, her thighs, and all of the parts that make her uniquely a woman, feel good to you, but after you've had the "feel good" experience, you're left with the consequences of your actions. The consequences mirror children, sexually transmitted diseases (STDs), heartaches, sad stories, and a truckload of regret.

I've met so many broken men and women. They were miserable, dissatisfied, and single because they chose to invest in what made them feel good rather than what was good for them.

When you meet the man or woman you may think is a good fit for you, he or she may not be beautiful by the standards of society. However, when they come into their own, they will lead you to a great, fulfilling life, and with that life comes a beauty that perfects as they mature and succeed in life.

What feels good to you will take you out of church, and put you in the backseat of a car. The relationships with your family will be damaged because you chose someone who made you feel good, over something or someone who was good for you.

Truthfully, I am madly in love with my wife because we live under absolute grace and mercy. We made all the mistakes. The wisdom and clarity you're ingesting comes from our real-life experiences.

God smiled on us, yet the consequences of our mistakes and poor choices have been very hard to maneuver through. If I started to tell you the consequences, you would think I was trying to get sympathy, so we won't go there.

While we are happy and well-rounded, life for us has not always been this way, and there are so many people we encounter who experience unhappiness.

Oftentimes, I think people confuse favor with the sum total of cars, houses, and great credit scores. For many, this is living, but when you get close enough to their lives you'll find their marriage and families are not worth desiring. It's not living at all.

Remember, people and things that are good to you, will never be better than people and things that are good for you. My wife and my family are good for me.

LOVE YOUR WIFE THE WAY I LOVED YOU

I never really considered the gravity of this command from the Apostle Paul.

Although Paul wasn't married (that we know of), he made a statement that seems like an impossible task to us as men.

I sat up in the bed when the Holy Spirit spoke to me. Paul said a man should love his wife the way Christ loved the church and gave Himself for her.

Still, I can't get over that revelation. So, I said to myself, he didn't tell me to love my wife the way I love Christ. In fact, Paul tells me to love my wife the way Christ loved the church, and the proof of that love is Him giving himself for her.

This love is so powerful because sometimes it's too hard for me to love Christ! I love Him, and I want to go to Heaven one day. However, there are times that the will of God, and the plan God has for me is stressful.

If I'm honest, I've had a few sleepless nights, and sometimes I don't want to follow where He's leading me. If I am to love my sweet Denise the way I love God, let's be clear, sometimes my love changes from day to day, week to week, and month to month.

Yet, Paul encourages us to love by using Christ's model.

I've had a hard life. There are times when I've felt alone, afraid, and mad at God. No matter how I treat Him, He always loves me, and He constantly tells me how important I am to Him.

The concept of loving your wife the way Christ loved the church is the only way to have an incredible marriage. When you follow this premise, real favor will find you.

The thing I struggle with most is knowing even when I act like an idiot, Jesus still tells me how loved I am, and He assures me that I'm His forever. Oh, what a love it is.

REAL FAVOR IN 3D

Years ago, we lived in San Antonio, Texas. We were young kids trying to make life and marriage work for us. I was a preacher at our large church, but I didn't have a lot of faith.

We'd just moved into this neighborhood with three small kids. One day, my wife asked me, "What are we going to do for food?"

We qualified for food stamps, but my pride wouldn't let me get them. We prayed for people in that situation, but nobody knew we were experiencing the same problem.

One evening I told my wife to put the pots and pans on the stove, set the table, and let's get together and pray.

When Denise Hall prays, heaven moves, and the earth begins the process of yielding. Within fifteen minutes of praying, there was a knock on our door. We didn't know anyone in the neighborhood, so my wife asked me to go answer the door. There, at the door stood the little lady from across the street. She asked me my name.

After telling me her name, she looked kind of embarrassed and said, "While I was in HEB, something told me to pick up a few things for you and your young family."

I was so happy, I wanted to shout for the one bag of food.

Looking at me, she said, "Oh no, I bought you a few things, then I got excited and bought more."

She ended up getting us ten full bags of groceries, with everything we needed.

What am I saying? The favor on our lives made her excited to shop for us.

One could argue we were poor because we didn't have money for food. However, the one thing we had was favor, and favor moved somebody that didn't know us into action.

Another time, my sweet wife wanted a fur coat. Living in San Antonio, there wasn't much need for a fur coat, but it was her desire.

When we left Detroit, everyone said we were out of the will of God because her father had a lot of money, and he would buy her anything she desired. People wondered why on earth her young and crazy husband would move her 1,600 miles away to Texas.

I didn't know she prayed for a fur coat, and she didn't want to tell me. Telling me during that time in our lives would have taken me over the edge, and made me feel guilty for not being a good provider to my sweet wife.

The people at home in Detroit were waiting to get the call that Tony and Denise were coming back because they couldn't make it in Texas, but we never looked back. One day we met a lady in our church named Sis. Aquino. She needed some things sown.

She asked my wife to the work for her; of course my wife agreed, and their relationship formed.

As she got ready to pay my wife for her services, she stopped suddenly, and asked "Have you been praying for a fur coat?"

My wife nearly fainted because at that time she hadn't told anyone about her desire—she hadn't even shared the desire with me.

My wife immediately began to cry. She shared her desire with Sis. Aquino. She told her how she'd prayed to God about a fur coat.

Sis. Aquino jumped up and said, "We must go find you one!"

We were poor, and we were thinking about the cheap stores, but Sis. Aquino told us no.

She said, "You are God's kids, and you deserve the best. The favor of God is upon your lives, and whatever you ask the Father, in the name of Jesus, He will do for you!"

Her words still ring true today.

I consider favor based on the scripture of Proverbs 18:22. Proverbs says, "The man that finds a true and faithful wife, finds a good thing, and obtains favor from the Lord."

I've heard this message preached for years, but I never heard it taught in a way that really satisfied my taste buds. Here's the revelation I've found resting in that scripture.

I believe when I found Denise everything within me was released and because we walked it through, I'm now seeing God's mighty favor on my life. Sure I could have married someone else, but they didn't have the key to the favor God had locked away inside of me.

I'm anointed to preach, I'm anointed to lay hands on sick people, and I have watched people recover. I am anointed to do business, and watch it succeed. I am anointed to raise good children, and watch them flourish. But, the truth of the matter is, none of that would have happened without the woman who had a specific key to my heart and destiny.

I've seen men with gifts greater than mine, and they were able to move masses of crowds. They've built great churches, and they have a lot of money in the bank. You would have thought with all of their successes, they should be living on top of the world, but a lot of them are successful in public, but defeated in private.

I tell young preachers before you get your fancy robe, alligator shoes, business cards, and meeting schedule—get a wife first. Love her until she finds the keys to your heart, and never open up to another woman that's not your wife!

I would not have been able to travel the world without a woman who told me what I would become when I was nothing. I never would have been successful or failed as many times as I did, but I got back up and tried again, if I didn't have the woman with the specific keys to my heart.

The reason I don't have affairs on my wife is because I understand that God gave every woman the same body parts, but only Denise Lenora Hall has the key to my specific heart. Everything I know about sex is from a woman who didn't make fun of me when I didn't know how to do it right, she took my fragile heart and taught me how to love her the way she needed it.

Today, I don't miss what's out there, because when I am intimate with my wife, I know that she is being blessed with the man that she taught to satisfy her need to be loved.

TOTAL TRANSPARENCY

I love my wife with everything in me. Whatever I am as a man and minister, she had everything to do with it on earth. Thousands of people prayed for me for forty years, but she was at the table with God, wisely building me for the past thirty-eight years.

When I found out about my physical issues, lost my eyesight for a few days, and started battling diabetes, high blood pressure, and other things—the biggest challenge for me is the thought of not being here for Denise.

I don't ever want to leave my wife. I am not afraid to die. I'm still alive because of my love for God, and the love I have for my wife. I can't imagine my life without Denise.

It's my desire that my sons and spiritual sons don't get caught up in the craziness of wealth, success, and earthly prosperity. My desire is for you to find your wife, build her up, and allow her to unlock a destiny that's in you. When that happens, you will fulfill every desire you can imagine.

A LETTER TO MY DAUGHTERS: NATURAL AND SPIRITUAL

When I was thinking about this chapter, I didn't want to leave you behind. As a father, I'm the only one who wants nothing but success and love in your life.

I say that because as men we are accustomed to asking in our head, if not aloud, "What is this going to cost me?"

Well, as I was writing about my beautiful Queen, Denise Hall, I also thought about you. I want you to know you are uniquely built to raise a man to go into the world and change generations for God.

One of the most important things you can have is not what's on your body, but what's in your heart. You MUST ask God for wisdom because wisdom will not only help you receive the man who will have you as a gift, but he will do whatever it takes to love you like Christ loved him.

Be careful who you open your mind, body, and spirit to because every man is not good for you. I know it seems like waiting is hard, but to tell the truth, getting the wrong man takes longer to overcome.

As a father, it is my job to love you, encourage you, get you ready to receive your prince, and most of all start the process of creating world changers for God.

This book has very little to do with what I wished Clarence Hall taught me, but this whole book is leaving on record the things I want my natural kids, and the hundreds of spiritual sons and daughters who call me dad, pops, Bishop, pastor, and mentor to know.

It is my hope that you have read this book carefully. I want you to take the principles I have shared and become greater than I have become.

If one of you reads this book and wins at life, then my living won't be in vain.

MY PRAYER OVER YOU TODAY:

Father, I pray that the men and women who are reading this book will see themselves in my story and make this book their life's manual. Using the lessons and principles of this book, they too can experience peace and joy, and help to move their generation to success in God. In Jesus' name, Amen.

CHAPTER 10
THE CONCLUSION: WHAT NOT TO DO

I've had weeks to contemplate how I would close this book. As I looked back over the chapters, I have learned so many things while writing. I relived the impact of my experiences. As I consider the weight of each lesson, I think the 10th lesson is by far the most important.

Sometimes life happened to me.

Sometimes I became a casualty of another's person's war.

Sometimes I was my own nemesis. Either way, each experience has brought me to the central theme of this chapter—you must know what NOT to do in life if you are going to obtain success.

I did not attend college, but life has taught me some lessons that have not only helped me, but they have also helped me minister to others as a pastor and spiritual father.

THE SIMPLE EQUATION OF LIFE

I believe in the 1+1 concept; it's simple.

When you do something in life, you are going to get something back from it. If you do good things in life, good things will come back to you. Of course bad things will happen to all of us, but we reap what we sow.

The grace of God will cause you not to receive some of the things you deserve, but it's immature to believe that simply because you love God you will never have any pain.

There are ten things I've learned not to do in my life. Life keeps changing, and time does not stand still, so in reality this list may change in the future. However, today, these are raw truths based on what I've learned from my eventful life.

THE DOCTRINE OF WHAT NOT TO DO

Learning what not to do is equally as important as learning what to do. I have summed up the power of knowing what not to do, and this piece of wisdom has taken me to some pretty powerful places in my life.

I remember preaching in a Chinese church one Sunday morning. I was pretty young at the time, and I thought I was going to knock it out of the park with the sermon.

After starting my message, I began to do my All-American style preaching. It was loud, fiery, and rhythmic. As I looked into their eyes, I saw a sadness that I will never forget. It was a message to lift and encourage them in the Lord, but my approach was offensive to them.

The pastor's thoughts afterwards were insightful. He shared that most of the members from China were a part of an underground church. In their church, they were unable to speak loudly and use American style preaching.

He explained that the members loved God dearly, but the older Chinese members just couldn't be a part of the larger service at his church because they waved the bible and sometimes pounded the pulpit.

I know some would argue those members should wake up and get with it because they live in America now. That approach would be all wrong. The next time I got a chance to preach to the group, I talked very reverently and kind, with no American rhythm, and the people loved me and the message.

That experience taught me the doctrine of knowing what not to do.

Was it comfortable? No.

Did I feel what they felt? No.

Did I leave there feeling like I achieved something? Again, no.

Were they blessed by the words I spoke? Yes.

You see, when you speak with wisdom, you move away from how things make you feel, and you get to the place where you are more concerned about the people you are assigned to help.

WHAT NOT TO DO IN MARRIAGE

People always want to know the kind of books I have read that have allowed me to have a great marriage. The answer is always the same. Each day, I work to master the book of Denise Hall, Volume 38. The volume number represents the number of years we have been married. Volume 26 is very different from Volume 32. I was able to decipher what to do and mostly what not to do. This doctrine has taught me how to deal with her seemingly different changes from year to year.

While reading the wisdom others have received is valuable, because I've studied my woman, I almost know what's coming next. I do however, read some material from time to time. I believe if I can read someone's book, become inspired, and take away key some points on success, then I can also study my wife, know what not to do, and that map will lead me to the things I should do.

For instance, I know I can be a pretty passionate person. I say what I mean, and I mean what I say. This method works great for me as a preacher, life coach, and pastor, but when it comes to my very sensitive wife, it doesn't work all the time.

When I'm upset about something, or I've had enough with a situation, I have learned that I can say anything I want, as long as I know how to say it to my wife.

I've heard men and women use the phrase, "get over yourself." Most of those people will never have an amazing marriage because they don't understand their spouse, their method likely leaves a lot of things unresolved.

My goal is for my wife to hear, feel, and understand. If I miss any one of those points, our exchange never goes well. My point is not valid if she doesn't hear, feel and understand what I'm saying. The way I present the facts are just as important as the facts. If she doesn't hear, understand, and feel what I'm saying, my time is being wasted, and we are not communicating well.

WHAT NOT TO DO WITH ADULT CHILDREN

I love my children, and I'm blessed to have four amazing children.

They are as different as night and day, but I love them all, and I am thankful God has allowed me to be their father.

While I love them, I will be honest, it has been a great struggle being their father in their adulthood. I have always been their father, pastor, disciplinarian, and the list continues.

Now, they are adults with time and experience under their belt. I've had to learn the hard way, the father that told them what to do and what not to do, has to allow them to make their own decisions.

Sometimes I really miss my girls coming to me for everything from advice on dating, to how to pick out a car. Now that they are adults, I've had to learn how to wait and be invited into a decision rather than giving my unsolicited opinion on a matter.

When I walked Felicia down the aisle and gave her hand to her husband (who stands at 6'7), I felt like my little girl was taken away from me. Five years later, I have learned that she needs me now more than ever, just not in the ways she needed me when she was a child or teenager.

Once, my daughter April and I went on a road trip. I came up with the bright idea to have a meeting with teenagers and their parents. I spoke with the teenagers on behalf of their parents, and April spoke to the parents on behalf of their teenagers.

Things were going well. The topic of what parents think about their stubborn teenagers was up next.

When April stood to talk to the parents, she opened by saying, "If you who are constantly bumping heads with your teenagers, it's probably because your teenager is just like you, and you can't deal with it."

Sitting there with so much pride in the fact that she was bringing it, I became distracted because her truth was a result of our relationship.

We always bumped heads because we are so much alike.

I can't tell you how much I miss those days, but she's grown now, and all that I have are our memories. Today, we are very close, but I had to reestablish the boundaries so I know what not to do as my baby walks into womanhood! It still hurts, but it works for us.

My son Tony went through a very painful divorce. After two years, we decided we were going to have breakfast one day. During our time together, he shared with me, for the first time, the real pain of his divorce. It hurt that he was no longer with his kids, and he could only see them every other week. It hurt that he wasn't with his wife. However, a lot of his hurt stemmed from my treatment.

He felt like I treated him with disdain. He felt like I ministered to him as a member of my church, not his father. Of course I led with a defense of absolutely not, but he told the truth from his perspective. As I listened to my son, I realized all he was saying was, *treat me like your son, not your project.*

His next words brought me to my knees.

He said, "You have always been my hero, and you taught me how to be a man. Now, I need you to let me be a man, make mistakes, and be there only if I need you."

His words went against my pride, and the feeling that I could fix his situation if he gave me a chance. But talking to me was not the 15 year old Tony that needed that father.

Tony, at 36 years old needed a father to watch and see the great things I put in him, and trust that he would figure it out. Today, Tony is rebounding so much better, not because of what I said, but because I gave him the respect as a man, and I did not treat him as daddy's little boy.

Darrell is a prime example of what can happen when you put all the processes of life to work.

Darrell spent most of his life incarcerated, but I believe he is on his way to a better life.

While I'm not his biological father, I am his "heart dad," and that is just as important. Because of the life handed to him, and how he chose to live it out, I thought he would never love or respect me. However, his words brought tears to my eyes.

He told me while he was incarcerated, he took classes in order to run my BBQ business.

One night after he got out, he waited for a few weeks before calling me. I was amazed that he remembered every conversation we had about becoming a man, how to change the oil in a car, how to treat a woman, and most of all of the songs I taught him how to play on a piano.

Today, he's standing at the threshold of 40 years old. Son, I pray you will use your testimony to help some other young men become great. I pray you teach them not to make the same mistakes you made in your life. You are on your way to greatness, and your mother and I are in your corner. We look forward to seeing the people you will touch because of the power of Christ working in you.

WHAT NOT TO DO WITH PAIN

I know it's good to pat yourself on the back, but in this lesson, I'm most grateful for the notion of what not to do with pain. I think this lesson resonates the most at 56 years old.

As you read some of my story, I think you'd agree, I've been through some tough stuff.

Truthfully, what you've read only touches the surface of some of the things I have experienced.

People who don't know what to do with their pain will get stuck. As life comes roaring at them, it will bury them with guilt, sadness, and brokenness. The reason I've been able to press ahead is because I know what not to do with my pain.

1. Don't let pain stay in your life long. Accept it, learn from it, and get rid of it. I have been through some hard times in my life. Once I learned the lessons from pain, I excuse it, and let it go because it is no longer welcomed in my life.

2. Realize the lesson may not be for right now. You can't coddle or nurse pain. The time will come when God reveals the purpose of your pain! I don't understand the "why moments" in my life, but if I let the timing of God have its way, over time, things start to make sense. Of course, if God

doesn't' reveal it to me I just have to settle with knowing God is in charge.

3. Change your attitude about pain. I view pain like a fever. I was told when I had a fever it was the result of poison leaving my body. When I have painful experiences, I view the experiences as God's attempt to make me a greater tool to help somebody else.

4. The best way to get over pain is to love. Jesus never told his disciples to pray for their friends because the only way to get past the pain that comes in our lives is by praying for our enemies.
   Praying for your enemies may not do one thing for them, or to them, but it will allow you to live in freedom. When I faced the pastor that tried to molest me, I asked for his forgiveness for my feelings towards him. I also asked him to pray for me; in that moment, I felt totally free from the pain of the violation, and the rejection that followed.
   I'm not asking you to go to those lengths, but I am saying you must get over the pain in your life. If you choose to hold onto pain, you will do nothing to the person that hurt you, but you will hold your spirit hostage and never become everything God desires for you.

5. Realize that some pain is payback for dumb decisions. This kind of pain must be accepted and dealt with directly. I have made some dumb decisions in my life, and I'm paying for a lot of those choices now. There is nothing worse than a person always griping over situations they created. I've learned this lesson because some of my decisions bred pain, so I have to deal with the pain that comes from my choices. Sure, God will help you through the pain, but until you settle your part, it will likely be a long, hard life for you. When I was 12 years old, I choose to smoke dope, skip school, fight

like a demon, and disobey my father. Well, there are still some things I suffer because of my decisions. Some things have become my normal, but God gives me continual grace to get through it, and my story has helped thousands of people. I'm sure if I had known better and the price tag for those decisions, I would have changed some things. Life is not like a video game where you get killed, and you're able to restart your world over again. Therefore, I will not complain, but I'll try to help others with my testimony—meaning, my life is not in vain.

WHAT NOT TO DO WITH EXPECTATIONS

Extremism is the death of relationships, so watch your expectation of others.

1 Corinthians 13:4-7

"Love is patient and kind. Love is not jealous or boastful or proud or rude. It does not demand its own way. It is not irritable, and it keeps no record of being wronged. It does not rejoice about injustice but rejoices whenever the truth wins out. Love never gives up, never loses faith, is always hopeful, and endures through every circumstance."

Once upon a time, I'd shake my head in disbelief, questioning, "How can anyone fulfill this kind of love in their lives?"

I realized this display of love is attainable if I have healthy expectations of people.

Because people are human, it is up to me to know people and base my expectations of them based on where they are, and what they can give.

So many marriages end with divorce because people have unhealthy expectations of each other. The woman I married when I was 18 years old is not the woman I'm madly in love with today. I think she's better, more beautiful, more spiritual, more loving, and most of all, more understanding than she was when we were younger.

Neither of us look like we did when we were younger, but we can count on each other because we know what our numbers of expectation are for each other.

As a young pastor, I was hurt so much because of unhealthy expectations. I was always hurt, therefore, I lived in defense mode. I was too young to realize that people are 100% of who they are, and they can be nothing greater or lesser. I held so many people to the standard based on my motives towards them, but people just couldn't live up to my standards. Now, I love people on their level. There are some people I pastor that are fully invested, and they love and support us. But there are others, who cannot commit to anything or anyone. If I try to get them to love me the way I love them, I'm going to get hurt and destroy others at the same time.

There's so much I have learned on this journey. There is so much I wish I would have learned sooner. I'm praying that you will start and continue the conversation. Although my father couldn't give me the things I needed, I'm a much better father for the things I have learned.

MY PRAYER OVER YOU TODAY:

Father, I pray the men and women who read this book have been challenged to open their hearts wider. I pray they will become the father, mother, mentor, or grandparent they desired for their life. Thank you for blessing their life, and thank you for allowing their life to bear testament to others, ultimately becoming a blessing to them, in Jesus' name, Amen.

AUTHOR BIO

TONY HALL SR.

Born and raised in the violent streets of Detroit, Michigan, Tony Hall accepted Jesus as his Savior at 15 years old. Although ridiculed by his family and fellow gang members, he accepted the call to preach at 19 years old. By 1985 he'd began to pastor in the inner city of Tulsa, Oklahoma, and he immediately found himself drawn to those with shattered and broken lives. After a few years, his journey led him to Houston, Texas.

Over several years, he planted churches throughout the inner city of Houston; he also established a Spanish-speaking church in the small town of Sealy, Texas. He has ministered across the country and abroad in Africa, Canada, France, Jamaica, the Philippines, and Spain. During those times, he ministered to pastors and leaders by equipping them with the tools needed to grow effective churches.

Using his life experiences and his years of counseling as a Pastor, he developed seminars designed to help couples rekindle the passion in their marriage. The Family First seminars have become an avenue to discuss real-life issues in a comical, yet practical way. He has been able to incorporate these seminars while traveling, and they offer hope to families around the world.

Tony Hall is an ordained minister and current member of Shield of Faith, Inc., an organization based in Pomona, California. The organization oversees nearly 1,000 para-church organizations around the world. He also oversees many churches throughout the United States, providing spiritual guidance to pastors and their families. He currently serves as the Lead Pastor for Conquerors Shield of Faith in Kannapolis, North Carolina. His love for people reaches beyond the four walls of the church. In 2013, he was appointed by Governor Pat McCory to serve on the board of the Department of Social Services, as Commissioner, representing eight counties in North Carolina.

Tony and his wife, Denise, currently reside in Kannapolis, North Carolina. They have four adult children: Darrell, Anthony Jr., Felicia (Andrew Bramwell), and April. They also have four awesome grandchildren: Anthony Q. Hall III, Danyella Denise Hall, Andrew Jacob Bramwell Jr., and Jaden Winston Bramwell.

www.facebook.com/asktonyhall

www.twitter.com/asktonyhall

www.asktonyhall.com

www.conquerorsshieldoffaithint.org

CPSIA information can be obtained
at www.ICGtesting.com
Printed in the USA
FFOW02n0508310116
20938FF

9 780996 630009